Bible Class for Adults and Youth: Beginner's Guide: Ecclesiastes

BIBLE CLASS FROM SCRATCH, Volume 21

Bible Sermons

Published by Guillermo Doris McBride, 2024.

While every precaution has been taken in the preparation of this book, the publisher assumes no responsibility for errors or omissions, or for damages resulting from the use of the information contained herein.

BIBLE CLASS FOR ADULTS AND YOUTH: BEGINNER'S GUIDE: ECCLESIASTES

First edition. December 21, 2024.

Written by Bible Sermons.

Table of Contents

Since it is very likely that Solomon was the author of this book, we know that it must have been written sometime before his death in 931 BC. The message of Ecclesiastes comes from someone looking back on a life of many experiences but few lasting rewards. As king, Solomon had the opportunity and resources to pursue the rewards of wisdom, pleasure and work. However, the world-weary tone of the scripture suggests that later in his life he reflected with regret on his past folly and wanted to guide us toward a better, simpler life, lived in the light of God's direction (**Ecclesiastes 12:13-14**).Ecclesiastes presents a view of life from a totally human perspective, but in the end the Master acknowledges God's rule and dominion in the world. The humanistic quality of the book has made it particularly popular. Ecclesiastes appeals to young readers trying to discern purpose and meaning in their lives, but also to men and women who have experienced more than their share of pain and instability, but who continue to cling to their hope in God. Ecclesiastes, like much of life, is a journey from one point to another. Solomon expresses his starting point at the beginning of the book, "Nothing makes any sense .... no sense at all!" (**Ecclesiastes 1:2**). These words indicate the utter meaninglessness of life as he saw it. Nothing could alleviate his sense of being lost in the world, for he had already tried a whole series of common remedies, from pleasure to work to intellect. It is useless to seek life without seeking God.But even in the writer's desperate search for meaning and purpose, God is still present. For example, we read Solomon's assertions that God provides food, drink, and work (**Ecclesiastes 2:24**); that both the sinner and the righteous live in God's sight (**Ecclesiastes 2:26**); that God's works are final (**Ecclesiastes 3:14**); and that God enables people to enjoy His provision (**Ecclesiastes 5:19**).

Ultimately, the great truth of Ecclesiastes lies in recognizing God's ever-present hand in our lives. Even when injustice and uncertainty threaten to overwhelm us, we can trust God and follow Him (**Eccl 12:13-14**).We all long for meaning in life. Often this quest leads us down winding roads, full of ups and downs, full of bursts of satisfaction that shine for a while but eventually fade away. In a way, it is satisfying to see this experience repeated throughout Ecclesiastes. Reading the pages of this book allows us to appreciate our common humanity. We identify with Solomon's journey because, for many of us, it is our own. When we try to make sense of things by seeking pleasure, working, or exploring intellectual depths, we all eventually realize that each of these quests is a dead end.Ecclesiastes shows us a man who went through this process and came out the other side with a wiser and more experienced perspective. Surrounded by the temptation to proclaim that life is empty, we find in Ecclesiastes a worldview tempered by experience and ultimately viewed through lenses tinged with divinity. Life is destined to remain unsatisfactory unless we recognize God's intervention. We must decide whether or not to place our trust in his safe and capable hands.*Have you struggled with misguided goals in life? Does your life lack the meaning and purpose you desire?* Listen to the words of Solomon and let them encourage you to place your trust in the Lord alone.

Introduction

To understand this book it is essential to know the meaning of two Hebrew expressions: vanity of vanities and under the sun. Vanity appears 37 times and indicates the useless, elusive and mysterious nature of life. Under the sun appears 29 times and indicates a worldly view of life. These two expressions indicate that the writer, Solomon the preacher, is not describing the world from his own perspective as God's chosen king, but from the perspective of an incredibly successful but worldly man who sees the world apart from God and concludes that there is no hope. Ultimately, the answer to despair is found in 12:13: fear God and keep his commandments.

God inspired the man whom he had endowed with the greatest wisdom (1 Kings 4:29-34) to write the book of Ecclesiastes (1:1, 12). Solomon wrote for the young men (11:9) and especially for his son (12:12), but what he wrote is useful for everyone. Solomon had almost unlimited resources to find the answer to the question, "What good is all his labor to a man?" (1:3; 2:24; 3:9). To find the answer, he explored many means of life: wisdom, pleasure, wealth, and even religious experience. After his attempts to discover "the good life," he came to a surprising conclusion: There is nothing better for a man than to eat and drink, and to tell himself that his work is good (2:24). In Ecclesiastes, Solomon gives many wise warnings, urging readers to try to live a good life. But the reasoning of Under the Sun leads to the conclusion that joy, wisdom, and morality all lead to the same end: death comes to all equally and is the end of all.

Could such a book have been inspired by God? Of course it could. Every word of this book, like the other books of the Bible, was inspired by God. It is the best example of reasoning under the sun, and it demonstrates conclusively that God's special revelation is essential to answer the questions raised in Ecclesiastes.

The name of the book means "preacher" or "one who summons the assembly". Ecclesiastes is read at the annual Jewish feast of Tabernacles. Solomon wrote three books of the Old Testament. He probably wrote the Song of Songs in his youth, Proverbs in his maturity and Ecclesiastes in his old age, near the time of his death in 931 BC.

The book of Ecclesiastes encourages the reader to look to God for the answers to life's problems and not to settle for reasoning under the sun as a means of arriving at absolute solutions. Ultimately, the answer to the meaning of life lies in obeying God and enjoying His communion.

Ecclesiastes 1:1-5

You will remember that when we were last time studying the book of Proverbs, we said that Solomon had been the writer of that book of Proverbs, and also of the book of Ecclesiastes and the book of Song of Solomon. We said then that Solomon had been the writer of that book of Proverbs, and also of the book of Ecclesiastes and the book of Song of Solomon. Here in this particular book we find something different from what the book of Proverbs said. In the book of Proverbs we could observe the wisdom of Solomon and here we can see the foolishness of that man. Ecclesiastes is the dramatic autobiography of his life when he was far from God.

The word Ecclesiastes means "the man of the assembly (or the speaker, preacher, teacher of wisdom or philosopher". We like to use the term philosopher rather than preacher because it can be misunderstood.

To correctly understand any book of the Bible, it is important to know the purpose for which it was written. You have probably noticed that we present an introduction to each book of the Bible that we study. It is necessary perhaps to go back, to move away a little from it in order to have a perspective of it. It is necessary for us to approach the Bible with a telescope, so to speak, before analyzing it with a microscope. In the case of this book, the need for this perspective is more evident than in many other books of the Bible.

In this book, we can see human philosophy apart from God, which must always reach the conclusions that this book reaches. We have to understand this reality of Ecclesiastes because in it we find statements that contradict other statements of the Holy Scriptures.

In fact, we are almost impressed to learn that this book has been a favorite of many atheists, who have often quoted from it. An example of this we see in the writings of Voltaire. Nowadays we find that cynics and critics tend to quote from this book. And it is also interesting to note the number of sects that use passages from this book and quote them out of context, giving them a completely erroneous meaning.

Man has tried in many ways to be happy without God and there are millions of people who are trying to achieve it every day. And this book shows us the absurdity of such attempts. Solomon was the wisest man who ever lived and he had a wisdom that was given to him by God Himself. He tested all areas and means of pleasure and happiness known to man, and his conclusion was that they could all be described as *vanity*. The word vanity speaks to us of something empty, without purpose. Satisfaction in life can never be obtained in this way.

God showed Job, a righteous man, that he was a sinner in the sight of God. And here in Ecclesiastes, God showed Solomon, the wisest man, that he is a fool in the sight of God. This is a book from which people of all cultural levels can learn great lessons. In spite of their wisdom and all their attempts to face life from an intellectual point of view, people who are not spiritually regenerated are considered by God as foolish. And this truth is difficult to accept by those who place too much emphasis on intelligence and the amount of knowledge and information they have been able to accumulate.

In this book of Ecclesiastes we learn that without Christ we cannot have true satisfaction; even if we were to possess the whole world and the things that human beings today consider necessary to bring happiness to their hearts. But today, the world cannot satisfy the heart because the heart is too big for that object. And when we study the next book written by Solomon, the Song of Solomon, we will learn that if we turn away from the values of this world and place our affection on the Lord Jesus Christ, we will enjoy the infinite beauty of His love, even though we cannot delve into its greatness. In this case, the object is too great for the human heart.

Again we want to say that the word "vanity" is the key word in this book, which is repeated 37 times. The key phrase is "under the sun", which is mentioned 29 times. And we should also mention that there is another expression that is also repeated several times and that is, "I said in my heart". In other words, this book contains the reflections of man's heart. These are the conclusions that man reaches through his own intelligence, through his own experiments. Although Solomon's conclusions are not inspired, the Holy Scripture that presents them to us is inspired.

We would like at this moment to present an outline of this book, since some conceive it as a collection of randomly edited themes. First of all, the problem is summarized in the following statement: "All is vanity". The exposition of this statement is found in chapter 1, verses 1 to 3.

Secondly, experiment, we see it carried out from chapter 1 verse 4, to chapter 12:12. By experiment, we mean the search for satisfaction in the following areas: science (1:4-11), wisdom and philosophy (1:12-18), pleasure (2:1-11), materialism or living only for the present (2:12-26), fatalism (3:1-15), selfishness (3:16 - 4:16), religion (5:1-8), riches (5:9 - 6:12) and morality (7:1-12:12). These were the things that Solomon tested, and in these pages he set forth his search.

And then we will have the result of that experiment, it is exposed in chapter 12 verses 13 and 14.

Let us now begin our reflections on the...

Chapter 1

Ecclesiastes is not a book of fragments arranged without "rhyme or reason", or a group of verses grouped in a random way. As we have seen in our general outline, it begins with a statement specifying the problem: All is vanity in this world. Then we find the conduct of various experiments by which Solomon sought satisfaction in different areas of human experience, such as science, the laws of nature, wisdom and philosophy, pleasure and materialism, i.e., living for the now, for the present time. He also explored fatalism, selfishness, religion, wealth and morality. Then, in the final verses of the book, he presented the result of his experiments.

Let us keep in mind that the conclusions of each experiment are human conclusions. These conclusions are not part of God's truth. They are the reasoning of the human being who lives under the sun.

Earlier we stated that Solomon's conclusions were not inspired, but that the Sacred Scripture that presents them is inspired. And we must understand what we mean by "inspiration" when we say that the Bible was inspired by God. Inspiration guarantees the accuracy and the words of the Holy Scriptures, but not always the thought that is expressed. In this sense, in all cases we must consider the context, paying special attention to the person who has pronounced a statement, and we must examine under what circumstances that statement has been made. For example, in the betrayal of Christ by Judas, the account of that event was inspired, but the action of Judas was not inspired by God. The same can be said of the words and actions of other characters mentioned in the Bible, who committed acts contrary to the will of God. Thus, what those characters said or did was accurately reported by the writers of the Bible, who were guided in their task of writing the text by the Holy Spirit. In our specific case of Ecclesiastes, the statements made by Solomon when he was seeking satisfaction apart from God, were not always in accordance with God's thoughts. Consequently, inspiration guarantees that what Solomon said has been faithfully and accurately recorded in the Bible.

After this general outline, which presents the general structure of the book and these introductory words, let us begin our reading with verse 1, which heads a paragraph that introduces

The problem exposed

"Words of the Preacher, son of David, king in Jerusalem".

We know of no other character in the Bible who can be identified with these words except Solomon. David had other sons, but Solomon was the only one who was king in Jerusalem. He was the philosopher that we have before us. And we know that he received wisdom. We believe that the wisdom that God gave Solomon was a little different than what we imagine. We generally think that he received spiritual insight, but the Bible does not inform us that he even asked for it. Solomon had prayed to God in the following way, recorded in First Kings 3:9, which reads as follows: "9Give your servant a heart of understanding to judge your people and to discern between good and evil, for who can rule this great people of yours?" Apparently, God gave him what he had asked for, namely, wisdom to rule. He demonstrated wisdom in political economy and probably exercised a good task of government in the nation. He ushered in an era of peace in the kingdom. Other nations of the world came to his kingdom to study and see the wisdom of Solomon. He gave a public testimony of God through the temple, with the altar, where a sacrifice was offered on behalf of sinners. These were some of the things that the queen of Sheba learned when she came from the ends of the earth. But in the area of discernment or spiritual perception, Solomon was probably nil.

Now, in this passage, we find Solomon, launched with his experiments "under the sun". And a man who lives "under the sun" is very different from a child of God, who has been blessed in the heavenlies with every spiritual blessing in Christ (Ephesians 1:3).

Let us continue reading verse 2 of this first chapter of Ecclesiastes:

"Vanity of vanities, said the Preacher; vanity of vanities, all is vanity."

Vanity speaks to us of an emptiness. It is wasting a life, a life lived without any purpose or goal. It means to live simply as an animal or a bird lives. There are many people today who live that way.

At one time or another, some of us have met at a hotel with people who have a high standard of living due to their financial resources. These are people who can satisfy all their desires, live in the part of the world that pleases them most, and devote themselves to the most varied leisure activities. But what is surprising is to see, from their conversations, the lack of satisfaction and dissatisfaction they reveal, as well as their degree of boredom. They seem to lead purposeless lives, having lost their enthusiasm and motivation for new experiences.

In the book of Proverbs Solomon presented us with jewels of wisdom. And in this book of Ecclesiastes he offered us globules, not of wisdom but of foolishness. Then, in the Song of Songs, the theme was love. Wisdom, folly and love were then his themes. Solomon was an expert on these three themes. He knew how to play the role of foolishness, he was wise in the way he ruled, and his love life was an intense story. So Solomon was the wisest man, but no one ever behaved as senselessly as he did. He is the enigma of revelation. He is the paradox of the Scriptures. The wisest man was also the most foolish. And this book of Ecclesiastes will reveal precisely this aspect of his personality.

We see that in the verse we have read it says: "Vanity of vanities, all is vanity". This statement refers to life without God. It is the life of man who lives "under the sun", trying to get something out of life itself.

So it happens to all those who seek satisfaction and satiety where there is none. They have tried everything to obtain it, but they only accumulate bitterness and disappointment,

So in these considerations of the book we will see the human being testing, experimenting. He is going to squeeze the juice that can be extracted from life, from the dry stones of this worldly existence. And in verse 3, the writer said:

"What profit does man get from all the toil with which he toils under the sun?"

Now, let us remember that this question is asked by the one who lives under the sun. This is man's point of view. God was not giving His point of view here.

We are now entering a new section that we have entitled

The experiment is performed

This experiment covers the main part of the book, extending from verse 4 to chapter 12, verse 12.

Now the first thing Solomon tried was in the area of science and he made a study of the laws of nature. It is interesting that Solomon tried this option. Men still penetrate the fields of scientific study and spend years, indeed, spend a lifetime studying these laws of nature. This book is remarkable in expounding these laws of nature. Let us then read verse 4, which begins to comment on these laws of nature.

Science

"Generation goes and generation comes; but the earth always remains."

Here he states that the earth is always the same. It has a stability that man does not have, because man is temporary. Contemporary man is a little different from the man of the past and will probably be very different from the man of the future, but he is a temporal being. And the continuity of mankind is maintained through births. That is, neither you nor I were here a hundred years ago, nor will we be here a hundred years from now. In fact, many of us may not be here for much longer. But, humanity will continue for generations to come. Solomon declared: Generation goes, generation comes. The human being is a transient creature. And if we consider this life only from the standpoint of life itself, we must say that man is the greatest failure in God's universe. He has been on this scene only for a very few years. In some parts of this earth there are trees planted that were already taking their place when Christ was on this earth but, after all, they are nothing more than newcomers, compared to rocks that have been here for millions of years, perhaps billions of years, we do not know how long. Although no one knows how long the earth has been in place, it was already where it is when man got here, and in this place it will remain after most of us are gone. Now, this adds a new dimension to life, which is a bit daunting; man is not what he thinks he is.

So we see here some remarkable statements that reveal that Solomon made a study of the laws of nature and had a great knowledge of them. It is interesting that these laws are basic in our time as far as science is concerned. Let us observe something else by reading verse 5:

"The sun rises and the sun sets, and hastens back to the place from whence it rises."

With all the resources Solomon had at his disposal, he found life to be monotonous. For him there was a certain sameness, a certain uniformity or lack of variety in everything he observed. These pages reveal that he was trying to escape that monotony. And people today are doing everything to add novelty, illusion, expectation to this process. People today are in a constant movement of searching for new forms of pleasure, of satisfaction, trying to get away from that lack of variety imposed by natural laws. if you simply look at the human being as he is today, separated from God, you find that he does not present a very attractive image. And that is what this book of Ecclesiastes will present to us throughout this study. But in the face of this panorama, we want to end today with another reality, with another image. That of the person who establishes a relationship with God through the Lord Jesus Christ and, in that way, although he or she finds on this earth the inexorable law of death, he or she will go on to enjoy eternal life. And in this new dimension, the children of God will remain forever. As the apostle John said in his first letter chapter 2 verse 17: "17And the world passes away, and the passions of the world pass away, but he who does the will of God abides forever".

Ecclesiastes 1:5-14

———

We return today to the book of Ecclesiastes and we will begin to look at what we are told in verse 5. We trust that you have your Bible and that you can follow the reading of these verses. We have already explained something about verse 5, but since this verse is linked to verses 6 and 7, we will consider them as a whole. Let us then read these three verses together; verse 5 through verse 7, of Ecclesiastes chapter 1:

"The sun rises and the sun sets, and hastens back to the place from whence it rises. The wind blows to the south, then turns to the north; and whirling on and on, again the wind returns to its whirling. All the rivers go to the sea, but the sea is not filled. To the place from whence the rivers flow, there they flow again."

With all the resources Solomon had at his disposal, he found life to be monotonous. For him there was a certain sameness, a certain uniformity or lack of variety in everything he observed. These pages reveal that he was trying to escape that monotony. And people today are doing everything to add novelty, illusion, expectation to this process. People today are in a constant movement of searching for new forms of pleasure, of satisfaction, trying to get away from that lack of variety imposed by natural laws. if you simply look at the human being as he is today, separated from God, you find that he does not present a very attractive image. And that is what this book of Ecclesiastes will present to us throughout this study.

So we see here some remarkable statements that reveal to us that Solomon made a study of the laws of nature and had a great knowledge of them. Interestingly, these laws are basic in our time as far as science is concerned.

Let us share with you a statement made by Dr. A. T. Pearson, who said: "There is some danger in trying to force the words in the Bible into a positive statement of scientific fact, in view of the great correspondence of certain statements. But it is curious that Solomon used language entirely consistent with such discoveries as evaporation and the movement of storms. Some have dared to say that Redfield's theory of storms is stated here in an explicit form. Without adopting this position ourselves, we may ask who taught Solomon to use these terms which easily accommodate the facts to the motion of the winds, which being apparently so disorderly and uncertain, are governed by laws as positive as those which regulate the growth of a plant; and that by means of evaporation, the waters which fall upon the earth are continually rising and rising, so that the sea is never full." And Dr. Pearson continued, "Ecclesiastes, chapter 12, verse 6 is a poetic description of death. The silver chain describes the spinal cord. The golden bowl is the cavity where the brain is located; the pitcher, the lungs; and the wheel, the heart. Without claiming that Solomon was inspired in predicting the circulation of the blood 26 centuries before Harvey did, is it not remarkable that the language he used was exactly suited to the facts, in mentioning a wheel, or a pulley pumping through one tube to discharge through another?"

We have in these verses 5 to 7, three very interesting statements.

1. First, "The sun rises and the sun sets". There is a monotony in nature, but we also have that on which we can depend. You can depend on the sun to rise, undoubtedly; and you can count on the sun to set, without question. We still use that terminology today, even though we know that rising and setting is caused by the rotation of the earth. We are resting on a portion of solid earth, and it seems to us that the sun rises

as well as sets. These terms have found their way into human language over the centuries. What is really surprising is the regular way in which the sun appears and disappears, obeying certain laws.

2. Secondly we are told: "The wind blows southward, then turns northward". Today we know that the wind follows certain rules. Even with the most advanced gadgets, it is sometimes difficult to predict the weather accurately. Recall that the Lord Jesus Christ said, in John 3:8, "8 The wind blows where it wishes, and you hear the sound of it, but you do not know where it comes from or where it goes." During certain times of the year, hurricanes and tornadoes form in different parts of the world. And they often hit populated areas. In many places there are terrible floods that cause the death of thousands of people. As Solomon said, in some places the wind is directed to the south and in others it turns to the north. In blowing, the wind obeys certain laws. Now, how did Solomon know this? He did not have the apparatus we have today, nor the background on which to base his conclusions.

3. Third, Solomon also said, "All the rivers go into the sea, but the sea is not filled." Solomon was tacitly talking about the law of evaporation, the rising of moisture into the air. Then the wind comes along, and drives the moisture into the earth. And so the whole process follows certain determined and specific laws. Nothing that happens is left to chance, even if it sometimes seems so to us.

So if we add to these 3 statements, the one in verse 4, and thus we have four remarkable statements about the laws of nature, which make sense, and agree with what human beings know today. Let us compare these statements of Ecclesiastes with other writings of the year one thousand B.C.; in them you will find many false and superstitious conclusions, which contrast with the accuracy we find in the Word of God.

And now we have another salient observation. Let us read verse 8:

"All things are wearisome, more than man can express. The eye is never satisfied with seeing, nor the ear with hearing".

This might not have seemed true in earlier times, but since the advent of television it is a fact of life. Many, many people watch television for hours, day after day. Why? Because the eyes can never get enough of seeing and the ears can never get enough of hearing. In addition, many enjoy traveling to other countries and meeting other people and seeing other landscapes. Such experiences are one of life's pleasures. I am sure that each of our countries has enchanting places, which we like to visit again and again.

The human being cannot exhaust the exploration of the universe. The more he learns, the more he reaffirms his need to learn. And this can leave a feeling of frustration. The physical universe is too big for that little human being. And yet, as far as we know, he is the only creature of God capable of understanding the universe. Sometimes we hear a dog barking at the moon. We don't think that animal realizes the distance between the earth and the moon, nor do we think it cares. We do not believe that an animal recognizes that it is living in such an immense universe. We think that animal's world is very small. But in the case of the human being, his eyes and ears are never satisfied and he feels the imperious need to explore. Then Solomon went on to say the following in verses 9 and 10, of this chapter 1 of Ecclesiastes:

"What is what was? The same that will be; what has been done? The same that will be done, for there is nothing new under the sun. Is there anything of which it can be said, Behold, this is new? It has already happened in the centuries that have gone before.

Some people think that the human being has produced something new when a new gadget has been manufactured. Well, we must insist, as in Ecclesiastes, that in reality there is nothing new under the sun. Even if in our time we use much more advanced means than in previous generations, it may constitute for a time, a novelty, which will soon be replaced by another and so on. And human beings will be able to share their feelings, their affections or show their aggressive reactions in a horse-drawn carriage of another era, in an automobile, in an airplane or in a spaceship. They will be able to communicate by primitive means, by radio, by traditional mail, by telephone, by Internet and other gadgets related to telephony and Internet. The environment may change and there will be new resources, new devices, new conveniences, and highly improved means of communication. But the basic human experiences of the human being will produce the same feelings, the same reactions and consequences. His spiritual needs, frustrations and lack of illusion as long as he remains apart from God will always be the same.

There are some people who said that the atomic bomb was something new in its time, but in reality, the atom has been in existence for a long time. The atom is older than man himself. Although mankind knew nothing about its existence for a long time, the atom was already here. All that man managed to do was that the atom became a very difficult neighbor to bear. Seeing its destructive effects and the passions unleashed by successive discoveries and their application to weapons of mass destruction, many would have preferred that man let the sleeping beasts continue in a state of rest and tranquility. But, again, the tireless search was evident. And in other different areas in the process of scientific exploration, great advances were made in the field of informatics and computers became indispensable elements in human endeavor. And those electronic brains, from a certain point of view, also contributed nothing new, nothing that had not already been created. Because God created us with brains that are highly advanced computers, and with nervous systems that are more complex in the transmission of information than electrical systems. Moreover, the human being is aware that the devices that he thinks he has discovered and elaborated, cannot bring him a deep and permanent satisfaction, something really new, that brings him a true peace, an inner tranquility.

But there is one outstanding exception. There is something new, called in the Bible the new birth. It is something that takes place in you when you receive the Lord Jesus Christ as Savior. And that is the only completely new event that can occur in your life, the spiritual new birth. Let's listen to the conclusions Solomon came to. Let's read what verse 11 says:

"There is no memory left of what preceded, nor will there be any memory left of what is to happen in those who come after."

In these verses we have seen that Solomon had tried to find satisfaction in the study of science, but he had to come to this conclusion. Man tries in every possible way to remain in the eyes and recognition of those around him. He tries to act in such a way as to perpetuate himself as much as possible in the memory of his fellow men, occupying a prominent place in the society in which he lives. But it is not long before he disappears from the scene, and within a few years his memory fades into oblivion.

It is true that some names have remained more in the collective memory because of the works they left behind or because of their influence on decisive events in history. But in the end, they have been less and less cited and replaced by the appearance of other characters whose names, in turn, will fade away in disinterest and oblivion. In this sense, we believe we can affirm that human memory is becoming shorter and shorter, due to the great speed at which names and events are happening today, to the point that we often have the sensation that time is passing more quickly. The Holy Scriptures say that we spend our time here on earth as a story or a story that is told, and that is not repeated, so that we can go through it again to evaluate and correct our successes and mistakes.

So we see in these pages that Solomon was conducting experiments of great importance, carrying them out in the laboratory of life. He was testing all the resources and experiences at his disposal, which were immense and reached to the very limit of human possibilities. In his time and considering the lofty position he held as king of an expanding nation, he could choose any area of human knowledge or experience. Nowadays, there are not many people who can have access to the means Solomon had at his disposal, nor capable of doing all the things he did. As we have seen, he devoted himself to the study of the laws of nature, but he found nothing that he could learn in nature or in science that was new in the sense that it would bring him new life.

In verses 12 through 18 we will see that Solomon seeks satisfaction in a new area. Let us then read verses 12 and 13, which show us that the king was going to experiment in the field of

Wisdom and philosophy

"I, the Preacher, was king over Israel in Jerusalem. I gave myself heartily to enquire and to seek with wisdom concerning all that is done under heaven; this grievous work God gave to the sons of men to occupy themselves therein."

Solomon spent much time studying the philosophy of the world. He lived about a thousand years before Christ and, considering that we live about two thousand years after Christ, it means that three thousand years have passed between that king and us. In that period, we can imagine the great number of elements or devices that the human being has produced in all orders. But, in reality, he knows no more of philosophy and wisdom than he did three thousand years ago. Let us continue reading verse 14 of this first chapter of Ecclesiastes.

"I beheld all the works that are done under the sun, and saw that all these are vanity and vexation of spirit."

All systems of philosophy lead to a dead end. You can make a similar experiment for yourself. You can spend your time studying these issues and you will surely come to the same conclusion Solomon came to.

We are living in times when educators sometimes think that past teaching methods were a waste of time. Considering the results, we ask ourselves many questions about the usefulness of current methods, which leave God out of the picture. Man cannot really come to know one really important fact: He cannot know God by means of wisdom and philosophy. His knowledge of God can only come to him through divine revelation. Philosophy generally leads people to take a pessimistic view of life.

You cannot take the normal human being, who is a sinner far from God, and provide him with an education of any kind, hoping that this education will solve the problems of his life, because it will not. Human wisdom cannot change human nature, nor can it correct that old fallen nature.

Only the power of God and the regeneration accomplished by the Holy Spirit can begin a work of control and transformation of that nature easily dominated by human passions and sin. Thus, speaking of his own personal experience and of the countless people he met, the apostle Paul could say in his second letter to the Corinthians chapter 5 and verse 17: "17So then, if anyone is in Christ, he is a new creation; old things have passed away; all things have become new."

Ecclesiastes 1:15 - 2:10

We go back to chapter 1 of this book of Ecclesiastes and we are going to begin our study with verse 15. Here we find Solomon performing a fantastic experiment, which he was doing in the laboratory of life. He is testing everything that was within the reach of man, looking for satisfaction and happiness. In his day he was able to go and test in any field of action and knowledge that he wanted. Today, there are not many men who could do what Solomon did in his day. In the first place, Solomon tried to give himself to the study of the laws of nature, but found that even there there was nothing of profit that he could learn. The same thing happened to him with science, in which he could find nothing that could be new, in the sense that it could give him a new life.

But there is one outstanding exception. There is something new, called in the Bible the new birth. It is something that takes place in you when you receive the Lord Jesus Christ as Savior. And that is the only completely new event that can occur in your life, the spiritual new birth.

In verse 15, we saw that Solomon tested philosophy. All systems of philosophy lead to a dead end. You can make a similar experiment for yourself. You can spend your time studying these topics and you will surely come to the same conclusion that Solomon came to.

The human being cannot know God by means of wisdom and philosophy. His knowledge of God can only come to him through divine revelation. Philosophy generally leads people to have a pessimistic view of life. Let us read then, this verse 15:

"The crooked cannot be straightened, and the incomplete cannot be reckoned with."

The first phrase we encounter is "The crooked cannot be straightened." You and I began life with an old nature, man has no way to straighten human nature. There is an old saying that goes, "A tree that grows crooked, never straightens its trunk." That is how it will grow. It will always be crooked because that is how it started. We can educate and do many things to improve but, as the Lord Jesus said in John 3:6, "that which is born of the flesh is flesh, and that which is born of the Spirit is spirit." It will always be flesh, and that is the reason why man needs to have a new nature, because, the Lord also said that, "That which is born of the spirit is spirit." That is one of the great principles of existence.

For a while we have thought that education would solve life's problems. Higher education, indeed all education, has been under scrutiny by a number of thinkers. There are others who have tried to come up with some kind of solution. Commissions in some countries that have looked at higher education have come up with the novel explanation that the problems of discipline and the low moral standards in many schools is because young people today are looking more deeply into things and are more interested in politics and what is going on in their world. Well, we will say that that is true, that there is a growing interest in those issues because we can appreciate the terrible things that are happening in the world. Media outlets such as radio and television gather a lot of information from all countries and broadcast it on the spot. This makes it easier for us to be aware, more than ever before, of what is happening in the world. Another example of the efficiency of information and of information technology in general is the speed with which the results of an election are known. In the past, it was necessary to wait several days to know the results of a general election. And what shall we say about the polls, which allow us to advance forecasts quite close to reality about who will be the winner and even the margin of advantage over the adversaries? Now, we believe it is true that people today are very well informed and aware of the current state of national and international politics, as well as armed conflicts, the rise of terrorism, major wars, the drama of immigration, trade tensions and the most serious problems facing society. But we do not agree with the implications that riots and conflicts in educational centers is a sign of progress because people are better informed and more aware of the problems we have mentioned. There is a deterioration in the aforementioned educational centers, which reminds us of what the prophet said in the sense that bad things were to be called good, and good things were to be considered bad. How can situations of evident breakdown of discipline and worsening of school performance be qualified as progress? We have to be realistic and define the situation as it is in reality and not as we would like it to be. We have to recognize that education cannot solve the basic problems of life. And many of the sciences that study especially human behavior cannot provide an answer, a solution. Those sciences have their respectable place as long as they take into account the place of God and the transcendence of the human being. Because the Word of God in its entirety contains, for Christians, the answer to the fundamental problems of life. Of course, there are no easy solutions. The study and application of the truths of the Bible requires a lot of time, discipline and effort from believers. And that is what is lacking for many Christians today.

Solomon then discovered that philosophy and wisdom did not provide an answer to the most transcendental problems of life.

Let us now listen to what the writer said in verse 16 of this first chapter of Ecclesiastes:

"I spake in my heart, saying, Behold, I am become great, and increased in wisdom above all my predecessors in Jerusalem, and my heart hath perceived much wisdom and knowledge."

We can say that Solomon, because he had a higher level of wisdom than the other kings, had come to have a certain arrogance and vanity. The apostle Paul wrote in First Corinthians 8:1, that "much knowledge puffeth up". If an individual comes to believe that he is smarter and wiser than others, or that he has been better educated than others, that thought can blow him up like a balloon. But, let us remember that education is based on experience, and experience is a fact on which one cannot rely. Experience must be tested against the Word of God. Unfortunately, many people today are doing the opposite, that is, testing the Word of God against their experiences. If their experience is contrary to the Word of God, then it will be only their personal experience, and not an experience endorsed by the Word of God. Then your experience will be wrong. And the writer went on to say in verse 17:

"From my heart I devoted myself to know wisdom, and also to understand follies and ravings. And I knew that even this was affliction of spirit."

Another version translates the last part of this verse as follows: "I realized that this also is running after the wind." Here we have the phrase "and also to understand the follies and the ravings". It is interesting to see that in the text of this passage, wisdom and the ravings of folly are not far from each other. Many intelligent men in the history of the world have been foolish. And Solomon was a notable example of this.

We think we have produced a generation that believes it is very intelligent. However, we cannot even solve the problems around us, let alone the problems of this world. Solomon devoted himself wholeheartedly to knowing wisdom, as well as folly and foolishness. He tasted both.

And verse 17 ends with the phrase "and I knew that even this was an affliction of spirit". In other words, the effort was not worth it. Let us now read the final verse of this first chapter of Ecclesiastes, verse 18:

"For in much wisdom there is much suffering; and he who adds knowledge, adds pain."

joy and satisfaction do not increase in proportion to the increase in knowledge.

"For in much wisdom there is much suffering" Solomon said here. The more we know, the more we increase our problems. Life today has become tedious, it has produced more tensions, and all the scientific gadgets that surround us, by the pressure they produce by forcing us to live under the pressure of great speed, sometimes make life almost unbearable. A certain man, a believer, once said, "I think I'm going to go crazy if I don't get away from these computers that are controlling life today." On the one hand we value these machines so much as instruments of work and entertainment, that they attract us as if they were objects of worship, on the other hand they are intoxicating us and driving us to a kind of madness, to situations of tension that are beyond us. How accurate was Solomon's observation when he said: "In much wisdom there is much suffering"! And let us keep in mind that Solomon did not know the era of the industrial revolution or that of technological advances. But he evidently knew what he was talking about.

Chapter 2

We come now to Ecclesiastes chapter 2, and here we see Solomon following another direction in order to find satisfaction in life. And that is the same path that many people are traveling today, seeking satisfaction and pleasure. He described this new search for us in the first eleven verses of chapter 2.

The pleasure

I said in my heart, Come now, I will prove thee with pleasure: thou shalt enjoy the good. But behold, this also was vanity.

We believe that Solomon tried everything known to man when it comes to pleasure. Our generation is sex-oriented. And what evidence is there of this? Depending on the context, there is a low moral level and in vast areas of the earth, there are venereal diseases in epidemic proportions. We must say that Solomon was an expert in this matter. He had a thousand wives. Look at that. Now, we do not believe that all of them were his wives, for many were what we consider "concubines". But they were all at his disposal. And a man who had so many wives or so many women at his disposal was bound to become an expert. And Solomon tried this way to get satisfaction. He also turned to drink and other forms of entertainment. Perhaps he could surpass many of those we know today who are engaged in these businesses. We must say that one of the things this man tried was pleasure. And his conclusion was "this also was vanity." In verse 1 of this chapter 2, he said:

"To laughter I said, You go mad; and to pleasure, What good is this?"

The king probably had a humorist or court jester to entertain him and tell him the latest jokes, and we presume that many of them were in dubious taste. Solomon said, "I found this to be a great waste of time." And in verse 3, he said:

"I decided in my heart to feast my flesh with wine and, without giving up my heart to wisdom, to give myself up to foolishness, until I saw what is the good in which the sons of men are occupied under heaven all the days of their lives."

As we read the phrase under heaven we remember that Solomon was a man testing and experimenting apart from God. And he said in verse 4:

"I undertook great works, I built houses for myself, I planted vineyards for myself."

These were all pastimes for Solomon. One can go to Jerusalem today and to other places, and one can contemplate the ruins of the stables that the king had. In the city of Jerusalem itself, there are certain ruins, and, also in Megiddo, one can contemplate the places where it seems that the royal horses ate. Solomon had stables everywhere in his country and this was something that was forbidden to him. That is, the law of Moses expressly forbade kings to multiply the number of their horses. Then, he said in verses 5 and 6:

"I made me orchards and gardens, and planted in them all kinds of fruit trees. I made me ponds of water, that I might water from them the forest where the trees grew."

He had an irrigation system, as you can see. And he went on to say in verse 7:

"I bought male and female servants, and I had home-born servants. I had many more herds and flocks than all who were before me in Jerusalem."

He had what we consider, a ranch or a ranch on the outskirts of the city where he could raise all these animals. Now, someone will ask us, "How could he afford those luxuries, or where did he get all the money for that?" Well, Solomon hoarded most of the gold in his day. He had plenty of money to spend, he wanted to have fun and build all the things that would provide comfort in his life.

It is now known that his servants fetched snow from Mount Hermon so that he could have cold drinks during the summer. And, we think that Solomon had tasted everything that man could do to achieve pleasure. We doubt that contemporary man can have anything that Solomon did not have, or an experience that that king had not already enjoyed. However, with all the means he had at his disposal, he did not achieve the desired results. Let us listen to what verse 8 of this chapter 2 of Ecclesiastes says:

"I heaped up also silver and gold, and precious treasures worthy of kings and provinces. I made for myself singers and singers, and all kinds of musical instruments, and I enjoyed the pleasures of the sons of men."

In other words, he had at his disposal the best actors, actresses and musicians of the time, who brought all kinds of musical instruments. With such a deployment of means, he must have organized artistic evenings of a high musical level. The performers must have played with their choirs and orchestras the best works of that time. However, these experiences did not bring satisfaction to his heart. And in verses 9 and 10, he said:

"I was magnified and prospered more than all those who were before me in Jerusalem. Besides this, I kept my wisdom with me. I did not withhold from my eyes anything they desired, nor did I deprive my heart of any pleasure, for my heart rejoiced in all that I did. This was the reward of all my labors".

Perhaps you have ever gone for a walk and looked in the shop windows of the commercial establishments in your city. Have you ever thought about how you would feel if you could buy everything you saw? Solomon was able to satisfy those tastes. Whatever his heart desired, he bought it, he got it. And when he looked at everything in this world, he was aware that there was nothing that could be denied him.

One would logically think that all human beings in that position would be happy. Well, we do not know why, but the truth is that they are not happy. If we consider, for example, the growing number of suicides, a first reaction would lead us to think that those who commit such acts are the people who frequent certain streets, where the homeless and vagrants take refuge. Because for many of them it seems that life is not worth living. But in reality, among that layer of the population there is not a high suicide rate. The highest proportion of suicides is found in the social sector that gathers the most wealthy people, the most famous people, and movie and television actors. And why? Because they have reached the same conclusion that Solomon reached, and are unaware of the beautiful experience of Christians who, having a relationship with God, can turn to him with confidence, to express their needs, their needs, their illusions, making their own the following words of the Psalmist David, father of Solomon, in Psalm 37:4, "Delight yourself in the Lord, and He will give you the desires of your heart".

Ecclesiastes 2:11-26

We return to chapter two of this book of Ecclesiastes that we are studying. This chapter told us in verses 1 to 11, his search for pleasure, as a means to find satisfaction and happiness.

We have seen a description of Solomon's pastimes. What we would call his life of leisure and free time. One can go to Jerusalem today and other places, and one can contemplate the ruins of the stables that the king had. In the city of Jerusalem itself, there are certain ruins, and, also in Megiddo, one can contemplate the places where it seems that the royal horses ate. Solomon had stables everywhere in his country and this was something that was forbidden to him. That is to say, the law of Moses expressly forbade kings to multiply the number of their horses.

He also had an irrigation system for his gardens. He had what we think of as a ranch on the outskirts of the city where he could raise all these animals. Now, someone will ask us, "How could he afford those luxuries, or where did he get all the money for that?" Well, Solomon hoarded most of the gold in his day. He had plenty of money to spend, he wanted to have fun and build all the things that would provide comfort in his life.

It is now known that his servants fetched snow from Mount Hermon so that he could have cold drinks during the summer. And, we think that Solomon had tried everything that man could do to achieve pleasure. We doubt that contemporary man can have anything that Solomon did not have, or an experience that that king had not already enjoyed. However, with all the means he had at his disposal, he did not achieve the desired results.

We have also seen that he had at his disposal the best actors, actresses and musicians of the time, who brought all kinds of musical instruments. With such a deployment of means, he must have organized artistic evenings of a high musical level. Where the performers must have executed with their choirs and orchestras the best works of that time. And taking into account the wealth available to meet the expenses of such cultural performances, these must have been real spectacles and pleasurable experiences for the ear and the eye. However, these experiences did not bring satisfaction to his heart.

To recall a little of King Solomon's experiences in the greatness and splendor of his kingdom, let us read again verses 9 and 10 of this second chapter of Ecclesiastes. In this way we will resume the thread of our reading:

"I was magnified and prospered more than all those who were before me in Jerusalem. Besides this, I kept my wisdom with me. I did not withhold from my eyes anything they desired, nor did I deprive my heart of any pleasure, for my heart rejoiced in all that I did. This was the reward of all my labors".

Perhaps you have ever gone for a walk and looked in the shop windows of the commercial establishments in your city. Have you ever thought about how you would feel if you could buy everything you saw? Solomon was able to satisfy those tastes. Whatever his heart desired, he bought it, he got it. And when he looked at everything in the world, he was aware that there was nothing that could be denied him.

One would logically think that all human beings in that position would be happy. Well, we do not know why, but the truth is that they are not happy. If we consider, for example, the growing number of suicides, a first reaction would lead us to think that those who commit such acts are the people who frequent certain streets, where the homeless and vagrants take refuge, people who lack the elementary means for life and see no way out, no solution to their situation. Because for many of them it seems that life is not worth living. But in reality, among that layer of the population there is not a high suicide rate. The highest proportion of suicides is found in the social sector that brings together people with greater economic resources, the most famous people and actors of cinema and television. These are people who are not beset by the need to survive because they have plenty of material goods, possibilities of finding pleasure, and friendships. And why then do they come to make the most tragic and irreversible decision there is in this life? Why do they feel compelled to flee this world by taking the decision to commit suicide? Because they have come to the same conclusion that Solomon came to, and are unaware of the beautiful experience of Christians who, having a relationship with God, can turn to him with confidence, to manifest their needs, their wants, their illusions, making their own the following words of the Psalmist David, father of Solomon, in Psalm 37:4, "Delight yourself in the Lord, and He will give you the desires of your heart".

Let us begin, then, with the reading of the passage assigned for today. Let us read verse 11 of Ecclesiastes 2:

"Then I looked at all the works of my hands, and the labor that I took to do them; and behold, all is vanity and vexation of spirit, and to no profit under the sun."

What a conclusion for a man who had everything! Very many people would not take Solomon's word seriously. They would have to make the same experiments, though not to the extent that Solomon did. Eventually, they would come to the same conclusion and say, "Life is empty." For his part, Solomon said, "All is vanity and vexation of spirit, and to no profit under the sun." How frustrating it must be to look back and recall the efforts made, the total dedication to a task, the time invested and the expenses incurred, and all to come to the conclusion that time has been wasted, most of life has been wasted!

As we will see in the rest of this chapter, beginning in verse 12, Solomon turned to another area, which we might call

Materialism

We would say that this is living for the "now", which should be understood by people today, because we say that we are "the generation of now". It is a materialistic concept. It is about living for the here and now, living for oneself, which is selfishness. Each of these words describes a facet of this type of life. Let us now read verse 12 of this second chapter of Ecclesiastes:

"Then I considered again the wisdom, the ravings, and the folly; for what can the man who comes after this king do? Nothing, but what has already been done."

In other words, no one could give himself the great life that Solomon lived. He himself said that they would have to repeat what he had done, and that they would find it very monotonous. And he went on to say in verse 13:

"I have seen that wisdom excels folly as light excels darkness."

Evidently, it is better to be wise than foolish. And it is better to be an educated person than an ignorant one. Verse 14 says:

"The wise man's eyes are open, but the foolish man walks in darkness. But I also understood that the same thing must happen to the one as to the other".

One can remember the time when you were in school and your teachers would say, "Think, use your head, use your eyes." And that is what

Solomon was saying here: "The wise man has his eyes open, but the fool walks in darkness".

And he went on to say: "But I also understood that the same thing must happen to the one as to the other. No matter how intelligent you are, you will not stray too far from the foolish one, because both of you will be taken out of your house feet first to be buried in the same way. And verse 15, tells us:

"Then said I in my heart, As it shall happen to the fool, so shall it happen to me: wherefore then have I labored hitherto to make myself wiser? And I said in my heart that this also was vanity."

One would think that an intelligent person could find a different solution than the one Solomon came up with "And I said in my heart that this also was vanity". Interestingly, contemporary man, despite the great inventions and scientific advances that have taken place in the area of medicine, has not been able to extend human life by very long even though the average life span has increased by about ten more years. But put those ten years next to a thousand years, or put them next to eternity, what do you have then? You don't even have a second on the clock of eternity. The reality is that the human being has not done much for himself here on this earth. Now let's look at what verse 16 says:

"For neither of the wise man nor of the fool shall there be memory forever: for in the days to come all shall be forgotten, and both the wise man and the fool shall die."

As you just saw, they die the same way. You may be intelligent from birth, with a high IQ. You may be educated, even have college degrees, but none of it will help you when the time comes for you to die. Nor will it prevent your death. When the time comes for you to die, you will walk right through that door, out of life, and there will be nothing in this world that will free you from that experience. Let us continue reading verse 17 of this second chapter of Ecclesiastes:

"Therefore I hated life, for the work that is done under the sun was grievous to me, because all is vanity and vexation of spirit."

Let us repeat that vanity means emptiness, it refers to something that is empty, without meaning, without purpose. What has been done with all that work that is done under the sun?

We can take as an example that great inventor Thomas Edison. He worked in a laboratory, and developed many projects such as the electric light bulb and the record player. All the recording instruments we have today are based on Edison's work. He was a genius, but he died, just like everyone else. And after all, all that brilliant work, what good did it do him, what good did it do him?

His laboratory is kept in Fort Myers, in the state of Florida, in the United States. If you ever go there, it is worth visiting his home and his laboratory. In that laboratory he worked day and night. He suffered from one of the best kinds of insomnia, so he had a small bed in the lab where he could lie down for a few moments now and then. He worked day and night, performing many experiments that never yielded any results. We do not believe that life was exciting for him. Rather, it seems to us that Tomas Edison found it very boring.

And let us listen to what Solomon said here in verse 18, of this second chapter of Ecclesiastes:

"I also hated all the work that I had done under the sun, which I will leave to another who will come after me".

Have you ever stopped to think about it? What good has it done you to have worked so hard all your life to accumulate some of this world's goods, and then you have to leave it to some relative who doesn't even believe in God? So many people have worked hard all their lives to accumulate some of this world's goods, and then they have to leave this world and leave it to some relative who doesn't even believe in God. There are many people who have left their assets to some Christian organization to use their money to spread the Gospel after they have departed. But many organizations have drifted away from the Christian faith over the years, away from teaching and spreading the Word of God.

For example, Mr. Harvard who founded the University that bears his name, Harvard University in the United States, was a faithful Christian, who believed in the integrity and inspiration of the Bible, and who upon his death left his money to propagate the Christian faith. Today you do not find that faith reflected in Harvard's curriculum, because its professors have turned away from the faith. So the money that Mr. Harvard left behind has come to be used in the opposite way that he believed, and for what it was intended.

Solomon had to face the same kind of problem, and First Kings 12 tells us what happened. He left the kingdom to his son, and it was his son's foolish arrogance that divided the kingdom of Israel between the northern kingdom (or Israel) and the southern kingdom (or Judah). That division constituted an irreversible tragedy in the history of the nation. Let us note now, what the writer said in verse 19, of this chapter 2 of Ecclesiastes:

"And who knows whether he will be wise or foolish who takes possession of all the labor in which I toiled and in which I occupied my wisdom under the sun? This also is vanity."

Solomon did not know what kind of man would take over the fruit of all the work he had done. And he considered it a waste of time to work for something and then hand it over to a foolish person. Imagine the tremendous sense of frustration he must have felt when he came to this conclusion. Let's see his feelings reflected in the words he wrote below. Let's read verse 20:

"Then my heart was again disillusioned with all the labor in which I had toiled, and in which I had occupied my wisdom under the sun."

Let us take note of the expression under the sun. It is a way of indicating the point of view of a human being who lives far from God. This is not the person whom Christ, from a spiritual point of view, seated in the heavenly regions, as the apostle Paul declared in Ephesians 2:6. That Christian person, contemplates the earth from God's point of view, from the perspective of the citizens of heaven who walk transitorily on this earth. But this other perspective that is defined as under the sun leads to pessimism, to discouragement. It is like staying in a dead end, on a road that leads nowhere. Let us continue reading verse 23:

"For all his days are but sorrows, and his labors trouble; for his heart is not at rest even at night. This also is vanity.

"This also is vanity" is the phrase that concludes this verse. And Solomon discovered something else. That it was not worth worrying about this matter, because there was nothing he could do to change these situations. Man couldn't do it then, and we think he can't do it today either. Then, in the final verses, verses 24 through 26, of this second chapter of Ecclesiastes, Solomon said:

"There is no better thing for man than to eat and drink, and to rejoice in the fruit of his labor. I have seen that this also proceeds from the hand of God. For who shall eat and who shall rejoice but himself? For to the man who pleases him God gives wisdom, knowledge, and joy; but to the sinner he gives the labor of gathering and heaping up, to leave it to him who pleases God. This also is vanity and vexation of spirit."

If you are living only for yourself, even if you are a man who serves God, or if you are an unregenerate sinner living for yourself, there is no goal, no purpose for your life, no fruit in your passage through this world, then your life will be extinguished with nothing left of it, neither here on this earth, nor in eternity. Being in that condition, his heart will end up full of bitterness, and he will arrive at the end of his life with nothing of value.

But, after this situation that offers no hope, there is another option that we invite you to consider: To recognize that we are sinners and that we need to appropriate by faith the work of Christ on the cross, receiving the salvation that He offers us. And then, by the work of the Holy Spirit, the life of the believer can be a fruitful life. The Lord Jesus Himself said to His own, in John 15:16, "I chose you and appointed you that you should go and bear fruit, and that your fruit should remain, that whatever you ask the Father in My name He may give you".

Ecclesiastes 3:1 - 4:9

———

Well, we come now to the third chapter, and in this chapter we note that Solomon adopted a certain philosophy for life, known as fatalism. This belief was common among the heathen; Buddhism is a fatalistic system, and so is Platonism. Today we find that certain cults give the impression of having great faith in God but, in reality, the "faith" consists of fatalism.

One can observe this on Fridays, when a large number of people return home from work. One can see these people, mostly tired, showing in their faces the weariness of the day's work. Some who are salesmen carry part of their work in their briefcases, and try to finalize a report, in order to present it on time to their office. They may have to mail it so that it will be in the hands of the President of the Company the following Monday. And if one has a chance to talk to any of these people, exposing their points of view, one will discover that many of them have a fatalistic outlook on life.

Once two men were traveling by plane and at a certain point, the plane began to enter a stormy area. One of them asked the other if he did not feel scared or fearful about the weather conditions. The other replied: "No, there is no point in being scared; what will happen, will happen, and you can't change it. If it is one's turn to leave this world, it will happen. So there's nothing you can do about it. And like this man, there are many, clinging to a philosophy of life that is quite popular. It is called by many different names, but its proper name is "fatalism." Many people approach life with this point of view. Let us then read verses 1 through 8, which begin the exposition of this point of view in which Solomon sought satisfaction, called

Fatalism

"Everything has its time, and everything under heaven has its hour: Time to be born and time to die, time to plant and time to pluck up that which is planted, time to kill and time to heal, time to destroy and time to build, time to weep and time to laugh, time to mourn and time to dance, time to scatter stones and time to gather them together, time to embrace and time to refrain from embracing, time to seek and time to lose, time to keep and time to cast away, time to tear and time to sew, time to keep silence and time to speak, time to love and time to hate, time to war, and time to peace."

This is Solomon's point of view, as he expressed it. In our time we often hear the expression "take life as it comes".

In one part of this paragraph he said: "There is time to seek and time to lose", so you can play or deposit money in the stock market and if you lose, well, that's what had to happen. It is observing life and accepting it in that passive way, accepting the incidents, the events, as they present themselves. It is the philosophy of fatalism. The Dictionary of the Royal Academy defines it as a belief according to which everything happens by inescapable predetermination or destiny. People who assume this belief show a resigned attitude, not seeing the possibility of changing the course of adverse events. That is what is expressed here in these words of the first 8 verses.

As we move forward we can see that verse 9, of this third chapter of Ecclesiastes, tells us:

"What profit does he who labors get from that in which he labors?"

What's the use of all this, what's the use of fighting? If you can't fight them, then join them. This is a phrase often repeated among people in various activities, especially used among non-Christian businessmen or entrepreneurs in the business world. Money is made on the basis of this strategy.

You will see that people who live with this attitude or way of functioning are not happy. We believe that they are people with whom it would be very difficult to live with. Verse 10, chapter 3, tells us:

"I have seen the work that God has given to the sons of men to occupy themselves with."

Solomon had looked around him: It was as if he had said: "I look around me and I see people with problems everywhere. I have managed to escape those situations somewhat, and I simply consider myself lucky, and that's all." Then, in verse 11, he said:

"He has made everything beautiful in its time, and has put eternity in the heart of man, without his being able to comprehend the work of God from the beginning to the end."

Here it says that God has put eternity in the heart of man. That is, he has put in the human mind the sense of time, the idea of the infinite. People have the longing, the desire to know the significance of themselves and their actions beyond time; they are not satisfied by being limited to time, to the ephemeral and temporary character of their existence in the world. There are many men who begin with this philosophy that they are going to squeeze the most out of their life in order to get as much out of it as they can. Solomon did so, and was not at all satisfied. Let us now continue reading verse 12, of this chapter 3 of Ecclesiastes, where it says:

"I have known that there is nothing better for a man than to rejoice and do good in his life, 13and also that it is the gift of God that every man should eat and drink, and enjoy the benefits of all his labor."

There is another group in this crowd of people we are mentioning; those who want to do good. A man once said, "Well, I think a person always has to try to do the best he can, he has to do good. That's what I try to do." That man wasn't doing much good, but that was his philosophy of life. Then, in verse 13 of this chapter 3, we read:

"And also that it is the gift of God that every man should eat and drink, and enjoy the benefits of all his labor."

This man said, "Well, I don't see anything wrong with drinking." And from his point of view there was nothing wrong with it. That is the fatalism of the contemporary human being. Now, in verse 14, we read:

"I know that whatever God does is perpetual: nothing is to be added to it and nothing is to be taken away from it. God does it so that before him men may fear."

They speak of God's will as paramount; but, with this view, man says, "Well, if it is not God's will that I should be saved, I shall not be saved." It is in this way that fatalism leaves no room for God's mercy and grace. Fatalism says that God does not hear and answer prayers. it is God's grace, mercy and love that make this life exciting, and that bring joy to life and give peace to the human heart.

At this point, we have another philosophy which we call selfishness. It is an excessive love of self; the self-interest of the individual is the supreme good of life. This section extends from this chapter 3 verse 16 to chapter 4 verse 16. So let us read verse 16, which begins to speak to us of the

Egoism

"I saw more things under the sun: instead of judgment, wickedness; and instead of righteousness, iniquity."

The writer was saying here that all men were evil. This is a cynical view of the human race, but we must confess that it is a fairly correct view of our human race. It is true.

A believing businessman says that many people, when doing business, trust the other person until he proves that he cannot be trusted. He says he has learned to treat people as untrustworthy until they prove they are not. Now, this is a cynical attitude. Unfortunately, it is reasonably accurate and we must say that our friend is a successful businessman. He confronts reality as God has described it. As the apostle Paul said in Romans 3:23, "all have sinned."

And Solomon continued with this line of thought. Let us read verses 17 and 18:

"And I said in my heart, God shall judge the righteous and the wicked: for there is a time for every purpose and for every work. I said also in my heart, This is so for the sake of the children of men, that God may test them, and that they may see that they themselves are like animals."

Now, this idea is not very stimulating, is it? And verses 19 and 20, they say:

"For so it is with the sons of men as with beasts: as the one dies, so dies the other, and all have the same breath of life. Man is not more than beast, for all is vanity. All go to the same place; all are made from dust, and all shall return to dust.

We are sure you will recognize that there are several cults, or sects, that are based on this statement. However, we must remember that this is the view of the man under the sun, who lives for his own self-interest.

Living for oneself, enjoying life for one's own pleasure, is the reason why people today get involved in some good projects. For example, there are many who are interested in sports and devote themselves to them. Others devote themselves to art, others to literature, and others to music or many other activities. These occupations are not bad, but they are selfish; they satisfy the selfish desires of the person.

This view does not accept the optimistic conclusion. It is that evolution says that man was a beast but has now become a human being. Selfishness or self-interest says that man is a beast, which makes the individual despise others. This philosophy produced the caste system in India, and the class system in other parts of the world. It leads to vanity and the feeling that one feels better than another. This philosophy has a pessimistic view of death; man dies as the animal dies. And since the human being expects to die as an animal dies, he will live for himself in this life and try to get all he can out of it. This kind of teaching is taught in many classrooms. Evolution is a form of it, although it says that the human being was a beast, and this idea that we have discussed says that the human being is a beast. It is only a difference between time periods. Both ideas agree that you are going to die like an animal, and that you have no soul or spirit, so you might as well live like an animal.

Remembering what we have just said, it is interesting to observe the behavior of animals. Have you ever watched kittens trying to eat? They have no consideration for each other. When they play, they play together without any problems, but when they are given their food, they do not care at all about pushing the smallest one out of the group, and then the owner of the cats has to personally take care of feeding the smallest one, as his brothers and sisters would be willing to let him starve to death, without worrying about it. Do they have no compassion for him? No. Their selfishness is also their philosophy of life. And one can observe the birds in their nest acting in the same way. Each bird takes care of itself. This is the viewpoint of the animal world. The reason why the human being is beginning to react like an animal is that he has been taught in school that he is an animal. Let us now read what verse 21 of this chapter 3 of Ecclesiastes says:

"Who knows whether the spirit of the sons of men ascends on high, and the spirit of the animal descends to the depths of the earth?"

Solomon recognized that man was different from the animal, because the spirit of man soars to the heights, while the spirit of the animal descends to the depths of the earth, because it is only an animal. And then, in verse 22, we read:

"So then, I have seen that there is no better thing for a man than to rejoice in his labor, for that is his reward; for who shall bear him up, that he may see what is to come after him?"

In other words, this life is all we are going to get. Again we will say that this is a contemporary teaching and we can call it whatever we want. In other words, this life is everything and the only thing that is really worthwhile is for man to identify himself with his environment and live as an animal lives. By the way, this is the old version of a philosophy that emerged from our schools many years ago.

We now come to the

Chapter 4

This chapter continues with the account of Solomon's quest for satisfaction through the philosophy of selfishness. And in the first verse of this chapter 4, he said:

"I turned and saw all the violence that is done under the sun: the tears of the oppressed, having none to comfort them; there was no consolation for them, for strength was in the hands of their oppressors."

Do you think this is somehow close to a certain political philosophy in some countries? Well, the egoist rebels against the system, against the ruling class. He opposes it. But whatever system there is, whoever is ruling, the poor will be oppressed. Frankly, the poor will always get the worst of it; there is no doubt about that. They are the oppressed. So the protest movements start from that social situation. Let's listen to what it says here in verse 2 of this chapter 4:

"I then praised the dead, those who had already died, more than the living, those who were still alive."

You may have heard it said: "I would rather be dead than alive". The person who says this is rebelling against the system and authority structures. It would seem as if death holds no fear for this person. Then, said the writer in verse 3:

"But I counted as happier than one or the other him who has never existed, who has not yet seen the evil deeds that are done under the sun."

And here we have the other side of the coin. It would be better if future generations were never born. Sometimes we hear the phrase, "I wish I had never been born." And verse 4 says:

"I have also seen that every good work provokes a man to envy his neighbor. This also is vanity and vexation of spirit".

It is interesting that the egoist rebels against the system, against the oppressor, against that which is wrong. But what can we say about the one who is doing good? And what about the one who is trying to do something about it? Well, the egoist says that's no good either, because it's a waste of time. Here we see that this is truly a pessimistic view of life. And in verse 5, we read:

"The fool crosses his arms and is consumed with himself."

Does this mean that the fool is a cannibal? No, it actually means that he is not willing to do anything to protect himself; and he will not even work for himself. Nowadays we have developed such a society; people are only willing to be given everything. Let us now look at what he said in verse 6:

"Better is one fist full of rest, than both fists full of toil and affliction of spirit."

And another version adds to these words "running after the wind". Frankly, this is a good statement. Of course, this individual only wants to do his own thing, what he is interested in. But it is better to have something this way, than to have both hands full of affliction or longing for illusory things. Then, verse 7 says:

"I turned again, and saw vanity under the sun."

Everywhere you go, you notice that things are going wrong. There is no way out. This is the worst kind of pessimism. This is a kind of philosophy that leads to suicide. This is the old sore that has become infected. Behind it all is the same pessimism of the philosophy of selfishness, which teaches that it all ends in nothingness. And in verse 8, we read:

"A man is alone, without successor, without son or brother. He never ceases to work, his eyes are not satiated with riches, nor does he ask himself: For whom do I work and deprive my life of all well-being? This too is vanity and hard labor."

What a picture this is before us! Even if you work for others and help them, you are simply wasting your time. And finally, said the writer here in verse 9 of Ecclesiastes 4:

"Better two than one, because they get better pay for their work."

Now he was going to give some good reasons for partnering with someone to form a team, but they would probably be selfish reasons. For him, two are better than one because they get more profit for their work. So you will be able to get more money by partnering with someone than by trying to go it alone.

We said at the beginning that selfishness was an excessive love for oneself. The person concentrates on his own interest and ignores the situation of others. But this situation of loneliness confronts him with his own dissatisfaction. And so, your only way out is to look away from yourself and raise your eyes to the One who did not shut Himself up in His own glory or in the perfection of His world, but moved into this world to rescue us from our sin and misery by dying on a cross. a look of faith in the Lord Jesus Christ will free you from that isolation in which you have shut yourself up, from your frustration, and will save you and give you the eternal life and freedom that all God's children enjoy.

Ecclesiastes 4:10 - 5:7

Today, we return to chapter 4 of this Book of Ecclesiastes, and we are going to begin our study as we said, with verse 10. We find ourselves in a section where Solomon, continuing his experiments in the laboratory of life and in his search for satisfaction, was exploring selfishness, living for himself. Selfishness is the excessive love of self. The selfish person is overly concerned with his own self-interest, not caring for the interest of others.

As you well know, the Book of Ecclesiastes reveals that Solomon tried to seek satisfaction by every means available to him under the sun, but none of these things gave him the satisfaction he sought, and he certainly did not find that satisfaction in living for himself either. But in this place in our text he was examining selfishness, and we find ourselves in this section that began in chapter 3, verse 16. We see as we come to chapter 4 and verse 10 the benefits of companionship. In verse 9 he had said the following: Better are two than one, for they receive better pay for their labor. So, let us now read verse 10, where he continued to expound the advantages of not living or acting alone.

"For if they fall, the one will lift up his companion; but woe to him who is alone! When he falls there will not be another to lift him up."

Solomon made the discovery that trying to live only for yourself does not mean that you can go through life alone. You need someone to accompany and help you. "Woe to him who is alone when he falls!" it says here. For such a reason we are recommended to form a group when we go on a hiking trek, rather than go alone. In case of an accident it is good to have someone close by. This is the problem of many retirees who live alone, who can fall and suffer a fracture, which makes it impossible for them to even go to the phone. Sometimes it can even take a day or two before a neighbor takes an interest in them. So, the writer concluded, it is better to be accompanied, because if you fall, the other person can help you.

That is, you can do many things together with another person, that you could not do if you were alone. And in verse 11 he said:

"Also, if two sleep together they warm each other, but how will one warm alone?"

In this way, one team member can provide warmth to another. Perhaps you remember when you were a child and in winter when it was very cold you liked to snuggle up next to your parents or siblings, to receive their warmth. So that, between the two of you, you could get warmer. Then, in verse 12, it says:

"One prevailing against another, two resist him, for a cord of three folds is not soon broken".

And while we're at it we can remember the well-known phrase, two's company, and three's a crowd. And it is good to be that crowd, especially if someone attacks you. If one alone is not able to defend oneself; it is good to have someone to accompany you.

In certain places it is not advisable for a woman to go alone to certain public places. She must always be accompanied by someone else.

As is well known, we have major security problems in relation to robberies and violence in the streets, especially in large cities. Often, the victim is the person who walks alone in certain places. This loneliness makes them vulnerable and defenseless. The Bible clearly teaches that people who are not regenerated by God, have an old sinful nature and, on the other hand, do not have the control of the Holy Spirit in their lives. It should be obvious that the civilized human being has not lost that nature and when he is influenced by his tendencies, or pressed by certain needs, he needs restrictions rather than freedom to do as he pleases. Generally speaking, the freedom that is often exercised in our time is the freedom to mug people in the middle of the street and in broad daylight, to attempt against physical security, to make calls with obscene propositions, to broadcast loud music that only interests a small group of people at hours when most of the neighbors need to rest. In other words, it is a freedom to express selfishness, the basest passions and the most destructive tendencies in any way and without any restriction. you already know that freedom is not expressed through abusive behavior. Our freedom ends where the freedom of others begins.

The self-centered person will not find satisfaction in this life. An individual working alone might find some satisfaction for a while, but would eventually tire of the monotony. And the same would be true of traveling or sightseeing alone. And verse 13 says:

"Better is the poor and wise boy than the old and foolish king who will not take advice."

In light of what we are reading about his life, we could say that King Solomon was a wise young man and, at the same time, a foolish king. And in verse 14, we can read:

"Even though he who came to reign has come out of prison, or though in his kingdom he was born poor."

Although there are many factors that produce the impoverishment of large sectors of society, it is unquestionable that corruption at various levels of public life in some countries, has helped significantly to make the resources of the most disadvantaged sectors of the population poorer. Of course such abuses and all kinds of abuses are contrary to God's will for humanity. They are a consequence of passions, of ambitions that human beings cannot control. Then, we read in verses 15 and 16, of this chapter 4 of Ecclesiastes:

"And I saw all who dwell under the sun walking with the boy successor, who will take the place of the other king. The multitude that followed him had no end; and yet those who come after him will not be pleased with him either. And this also is vanity and vexation of spirit".

Let's look at the phrase "the successor boy, who will take the place of the other king". It is interesting to remember that Solomon was the second son of Bathsheba (David's wife) and he was not the person David would have chosen to be king. And Solomon had apparently realized this. We should also mention that Isaac was not Abraham's first son, nor was Jacob Isaac's firstborn son. God sometimes fulfilled his purpose by choosing those who were second class. if you think you are a second class person, remember that before God, you are a first class person.

Then, the second thing to notice here is that as we move on in time, things look different from what they were at first. It says here "those who come after him will not be happy with him either". Sometimes a president begins his term of office surrounded by popularity, but as time goes by, sometimes because of the performance of his administration or because of the wear and tear of the work of government, his level of acceptance decreases until it reaches the point where a part of the population considers that his government measures harm a nation, leading it towards decadence. That is why this verse 16 says: "The multitude that followed him had no end; and yet those who come after him will not be happy with him either".

And now, in our study of Ecclesiastes, we come to the

Chapter 5

At this point in the story Solomon continued his search and tried something else, and that attempt might interest many today. He tried to find satisfaction in religion and did not find it. We are going to say some things here that may surprise you, but we beg you not to reject them until you have considered them carefully.

The nature of human beings, specifically their passions, have led many people to become fanatical, to defend their religious or political beliefs or opinions with excessive tenacity. In the name of religion, the greatest abuses have been committed, the worst abuses, and cruel wars have been waged. Did you know that this way of understanding religion has harmed more people in this world than anything else? Let us remember what the practitioners of pagan religions have done for people throughout Biblical history.

On the other hand, we can observe that when certain theological trends have promoted views affecting the authority of the Bible and the relative character of the Word of God, a deterioration of the spiritual level of Christians is produced, as well as a disinterest in the diffusion of the Bible and the proclamation of the Gospel message.

Rather than trying to have a religion, what human beings need is to have Christ. From our point of view one could not call Christianity a religion. The Bible does not establish a set of rules for celebrating religious ceremonies. For this reason there is a great diversity of Christian congregations that practice various forms of worship. Christianity was not given a ritual rule to follow, because from the beginning it was centered on a Person, that is, Christ. To be a Christian means that one trusts in Christ. Religious practice, by itself, never helped man very much.

Let us listen to this tremendous statement that Solomon uttered in the first verse of this chapter 5 when he found himself

Seeking satisfaction in religion

"When you go to the house of God, watch your step. Come nearer to hear than to offer the sacrifice of fools, who know not that they do wrong."

Solomon tried to become a religious person and went to the temple. Here is a word of caution to pronounce hasty vows or promises. And he went on to say in verse 2:

"Be not hasty to open thy mouth, neither let thine heart be hasty to utter a word before God: for God is in heaven, and thou upon earth. Therefore let your words be few."

The warning is directed against making decisions under the pressure of emotions. The writer had tried this superficial religiosity. And there are many unhappy Christians today. They never commit themselves. They are content to comply with a comfortable, brief and pleasant ritual. There is nothing that dulls the spiritual life more than that kind of apparent religiosity. And he went on to say in verse 3:

"For out of many occupations come dreams, and out of the multitude of words the voice of the fool."

The foolish often express themselves with a great abundance of words. And these words should not be uttered in the presence of the Lord. And the writer said in verse 4:

"When you make a promise to God, do not delay in keeping it, for he has no pleasure in fools. Fulfill what you promise."

When an invitation is extended in a church to promise something to God, one should not respond to it simply by feeling excited or impressed by the atmosphere. He will have to feel an inner conviction by the Holy Spirit. One cannot promise God something lightly or be dragged along by the attitude of others. One cannot expect to renege on something promised to God and pretend to continue to maintain a vital relationship with Him, a relationship of fellowship and communion enjoying God's blessing. Then Solomon went on to say in verses 5 and 6:

"It is better not to promise than to promise and not perform. Let not your mouth make you sin, nor before the angel say that it was out of ignorance: why make God angry because of your words, and destroy the work of your hands?"

Did you know that God gave a law concerning this matter? Chapter 27 of the Book of Leviticus dealt with the subject of promises. God gave certain laws concerning promises. When you make any deal with God, you had better keep what you say, because God will take your word for it and hold you accountable for it. Some do not seem to realize that we are dealing with a living, real God, attentive to our words and thoughts, and they live apart from God's will. We should take our dealings with God very seriously. It says here that a hasty promise produces displeasure in God, and may result in the destruction of what someone has done, of the fruit of his labor. And so, it will have been shown that such work, such activities were futile, useless. They did not constitute a work destined to remain. And let us observe how the writer illustrated what he meant. Let us continue reading verse 7:

"For where dreams abound, vanities and many words abound also. But you, fear God."

Solomon compared hasty vows or promises to dreams, or to nightmares that have no meaning. And in this context, they are considered vanities, and foolish talk. In the midst of so many foolish words, the writer exhorts us to have a reverent, respectful fear of God.

There is no element in life that can substitute for a personal relationship with God. Some use their personal experiences to test the Word of God. And the process should be exactly the opposite. Every experience should be put to the test, contrasted with the Word of God. In this regard we must remember a significant passage in the New Testament, in the first letter of the apostle John chapter 4, verse 1, which says: "Beloved, do not believe every spirit, but test the spirits to see whether they are from God, because many false prophets have gone out into the world". Many people go off on a tangent of experience and live supported by it. That is just another form of religiosity. It is an appeal to the emotions or to the aesthetic sense.

Does your faith in Christ rest on a series of specific experiences, or on the Word of God? Does it depend on certain formalisms or habits? Does it depend only on your state of mind, or on your emotions? Or rather, do you have Christ? Keep in mind that the Lord Jesus Christ, who is the living Word of God, who became incarnate and came into this world to die for us, gives eternal life to all those who by faith accept His work of redemption on the cross, thus becoming children of God. But we are not only talking about eternal life beyond death. God's children have within their reach enormous spiritual resources through the work of God's Spirit. God is pleased to give each of His children a new motivation for living, new goals. Those who seek their satisfaction in Him and in the fulfillment of His will, will enjoy His guidance, His direction in the circumstances of their lives, and the strength necessary to lead a purposeful life. The Christian's guide and orientation, therefore, is the Word of God, which is the basis of his hope and the foundation of all his experiences. And, by the way, the experiences that the work of the Holy Spirit brings to our lives cannot be compared to any human experience, devised or elaborated by human projects or ideas. Many speak today of increasing the quality of their life, thinking rather of acquiring the material elements that provide that comfort, that economic relief that frees us from economic pressure. But all human means are useless to bring to the human heart an integral and lasting satisfaction. For all these reasons and in contrast, the experiences that the Word of God and the Holy Spirit bring to a life constitute the highest exponent of quality of life that can be achieved on this earth. And that is the quality of life we desire for you.

Ecclesiastes 5:8 - 6:12

We find ourselves in a section of the book of Ecclesiastes where Solomon was seeking satisfaction through religion. You will remember that Solomon was conducting an experiment in life itself. Probably the only man who could have conducted this kind of experiment because of the great resources at his disposal. He had tried to find contentment in life through the study of science, natural laws; wisdom and philosophy, pleasure, materialism, that is, living for the present. And then he tried to take on fatalism, which is today a rather popular way of looking at life. Also egoism; that is, living for oneself. And, then, this man also tried religion. Now, this does not mean that he tested God, because he did not. We saw that he discovered that if you go through certain forms or rituals, they are not going to satisfy you in your heart, and that you must be careful when dealing with God in making promises to Him because He is a reality, and He will deal with you in a very definite way. Now, in verse 7 of chapter 5, of Ecclesiastes, we read:

"For where dreams abound, vanities and many words abound also. But you, fear God."

Solomon compared hasty vows or promises to dreams, or to nightmares that have no meaning. And in this context, they are considered vanities, and absurd talk. And in the midst of so many foolish words, the writer exhorted us to have a reverent, respectful fear of God. There is no element in life that can substitute for a personal relationship with God. Some use their personal experiences to test the Word of God. And the process should be exactly the opposite. Every experience should be put to the test, contrasted with the Word of God. In this regard we must remember a significant passage in the New

Testament, in the first letter of the apostle John chapter 4, verse 1, which says: "Beloved, do not believe every spirit, but test the spirits to see whether they are from God, because many false prophets have gone out into the world". Many people go off on a tangent of experience and live supported by it. That is just another form of religiosity. It is an appeal to the emotions or to the aesthetic sense.

Does your faith in Christ rest on a series of specific experiences, or on the Word of God? Does it depend on certain formalisms or habits? Does it depend solely on your state of mind, or on your emotions? Or rather, do you have Christ?

Let us now read verse 8 of this fifth chapter of Ecclesiastes, in which Solomon said:

"If you see in the province that the poor are oppressed and right and justice are perverted, do not marvel; for over one high one watches over another higher, and a higher one is over both."

In some countries and even in international organizations there is corruption in special programs to help the poor, because many today are trying to enrich themselves at the expense of the least favored in society. But God will judge these situations. Here in this verse it says: "For a higher one watches over a higher one". God sees what is happening and will deal with that abuse and injustice with severity.

The history of this world confirms this. God is aware of the way in which some governments or organizations approach this help to the needy. There have been governments that have tried to abuse the poor and those governments have fallen. In some cases the fall has been violent, traumatic. It was really God's judgment on a widespread state of corruption in which a few were living at the expense of many in need.

God has a lot to say about helping the poor. When the Lord Jesus comes to reign during the kingdom age, people will find that there is Someone reigning who means it when He says He is going to do something for the poor. There will be justice and fairness for them. We don't think He will put them on a dole system. But each person will make his contribution and get a fair deal.

Now, this brings us to the next division in the account of the experiments Solomon undertook to find satisfaction in life. As we have seen, he tried science, the study of natural laws. He tried wisdom and philosophy, pleasure and materialism. He tried to live only for the present. He also tried fatalism and selfishness, that is, living only for himself. And after all these things, he tried religion.

Now we will see Solomon engage in another experiment. He was in a position to obtain and enjoy wealth more than anyone else. In his time, he was probably the richest man on earth. He devoted himself to accumulating gold and was able to get everything he wanted. Solomon's riches were the factor that finally caused the downfall of the nation. The greed of the nations around him was aroused and they moved to get some of that wealth. God had placed a wall of protection around Israel but that wall crumbled. And God then allowed those nations to enter Israel to take advantage of that wealth. Let's read then verse 10, chapter 5, where we see the writer began to talk about

The pursuit of satisfaction in the attainment and enjoyment of wealth

"He that loveth money shall not be satisfied with money; and he that loveth riches shall not bring forth fruit. This also is vanity."

We can imagine the president of a large company who at the end of the fiscal year finds that he has accumulated a large profit, but this fact will not really satisfy him. A person may have a large bank account, which offers some measure of security, but it will not really satisfy him. Riches will not bring satisfaction in life.

There is nothing wrong with wealth in itself. The Bible never condemns wealth, yes, it condemns the love of money. Not money itself. The problem is the love of money, which is the root of all evil (as we see in 1 Timothy 6:10). To accumulate wealth just for the sake of accumulating wealth is wrong. It has been said that the miser thinks that bills are flat so that he can stack them, while the spendthrift thinks that money is round so that he can roll it around. Both are totally wrong.

A man's attitude toward money is the point at issue. There is nothing wrong with the very profit system in place today. What is wrong is located in the people who are involved in the system. What is wrong is the love of money. The love of money makes people try to be rich for the sake of being rich.

And one can see people who have come together, bound by an agreement, to make money simply for that reason alone. On one occasion, a comedian was making a public presentation about a play in whose production he had taken part. He was expressing his thanks to all those who had participated and explaining to what extent they had all collaborated. It was a well-prepared speech without the slightest trace of humor. And as he came to the end he said, "And we have all stood together in this effort for one reason only," he paused and added, "greed!" And that had been the case. Greed had been the ingredient that kept them together to make that production. And that is the ingredient that holds many individuals and organizations together.

In certain regions of the world one can observe some countries where a leader is allowed to become immeasurably rich while the rest of the inhabitants of that nation live in abject poverty. God condemns these sad situations. And He condemns it because of the love of money that it implies in some, and because of the use they make of that money. And what is condemnable is that passion for money, regardless of the political orientation or the system that governs a country. How different our society and the world would be, if human beings produced money and profits for the honor and glory of God! If people would work for money motivated by the honor and glory of God. It would be beautiful if money were used in the right way. But, of course, in the face of such a strong and deep-rooted passion, the only cure for greed is to experience an encounter with Christ, is to have Him in the heart.

Let us now continue reading verse 11 of this fifth chapter of Ecclesiastes:

"When goods increase, those who consume them also increase. What benefit, then, will their owner have, other than to see them with his own eyes?"

Growth for growth's sake is not good. This is true in business, in Christian organizations and in the church.

The author of these Bible studies, Dr. J. Vernon McGee, said that for years he was the pastor of a large church. He soon discovered that growing for the sake of growing, to have a large church membership, was nothing but a source of trouble. It was not an activity to be enjoyed, or something to rejoice about. He said that the Lord taught him that growing for the honor and glory of God had to be the sole purpose of life. And he said that he put this lesson into practice by having this goal before him and devoted himself with renewed enthusiasm to spreading the Word of God.

Well, let's move on now; in verse 12 of this chapter 5 we read:

"Sweet is the sleep of the laborer, whether he eats much or eats little; but the rich man is not allowed to sleep by abundance."

While the one who works always sleeps peacefully and at ease, the rich man must always be on guard to protect his wealth from those who would take it away from him, or from those who would otherwise threaten his business and the source of his income. Obsessive thinking about it all keeps him awake at night.

Once a very rich lady was in a hotel, where the clients were asked to deposit their valuables in the hotel safe so that they would be better protected. And this very rich lady deposited in the hotel safe her jewelry, and she had so many things that it took her about 30 minutes to do it. The young lady in charge of this task said, "That lady has been here before, and she will come down here to this office a dozen times to check if all her jewelry is in and to take some out to wear; and then she brings it back." That woman had, indeed, a big problem, and her preoccupation with the riches she carried with her did not allow her to fully enjoy the beauty of the place she was in. We can see then that there are many reasons why the rich man does not allow him to sleep in abundance.

Let us now see what verse 13 says:

"There is a sore evil I have seen under the sun: riches kept by their owners for their own evil."

Wealth actually hurts rather than helps many people. As we have just seen, sometimes people who possess fewer resources are happier than those who possess great wealth. However, the Apostle Paul said in Philippians 4:12, that he knew how to live in abundance, and what it was like to live in poverty. Frankly speaking, we would like to try both options. Now, verse 14, speaking of riches says:

"Which are wasted by misuse, and the son whom they have begotten has nothing left in his hand."

That is to say that a person can accumulate a fortune and leave it to his son and he could spend it all. But in some countries, there are people who, intelligently, do not leave the money directly under the control of the children. They leave it, for example, in the hands of a lawyer, a trustee or some other trustworthy person, to distribute it among the children in small amounts, in order to protect the family fortune.

On the other hand, there are people who never made any money during their lifetime. They are wealthy people because they once received an inheritance. But they lack wisdom and discernment about how to use the money they have. Sometimes these people are in positions of influence. This fact could be a problem or not, depending on whether they use their money judiciously and with good motivation.

We believe that the division of society in some nations is not primarily caused by race. Rather, it comes down to the traditional division between rich and poor. This has always been the line of demarcation down through the centuries. Solomon seems to have understood the problems that factors such as corruption, bad investments, wastefulness, and the accumulation and retention of money would have for the economy and for those in control of capital. What became clear to him was that riches, by themselves, do not satisfy the cravings of the human soul, they do not constitute a solution to the problems of life. And so we come to

Chapter 6

This chapter concludes the section of the book in which we can see his conclusions from his experiences in obtaining and enjoying the immense riches he possessed, in his quest for contentment. Let us then read verses 1 and 2 of this sixth chapter of Ecclesiastes:

"There is an evil which I have seen under heaven, and it is very common among men: that of the man to whom God gives riches, goods, and honor, and he lacks nothing of all that his soul desires; but God gives him no faculty to enjoy it, but strangers enjoy it. This is vanity and painful evil".

A friend of Professor McGee's told him that on one occasion, while staying at a hotel in Florida, he saw the elderly billionaire John Rockefeller sitting at his table having dinner. His dinner was very light, appropriate to the rigorous diet he had to follow because of his health problems. A little farther away and in a corner, one of the hotel waiters was also dining; in front of him was a plate with a well-seasoned piece of meat and other gastronomic delicacies. Both men offered to the eye an interesting contrast, revealing the immense social distance that separated them. The man who could afford the most complete and expensive dish in the luxurious restaurant, could not enjoy it. And the waiter, who normally could not afford such a dish, could eat it because he was in good health and also worked in the restaurant. Now, verse 3 of this chapter 6, of Ecclesiastes says:

> *"Though a man beget a hundred children, and live many years, and the days of his age be many, if his soul be not satisfied with good, and moreover he lacked burial, I say that he had better have an abortifacient."*

The uselessness and pitifulness of riches not enjoyed are here considered worse than the tragedy of the unborn. And when his life ends with the arrival of death, he will be able to take nothing with him. It has been popularly said that the shroud has no pockets. Let us remember the life of the patriarch Job. He said that he had come into this world with nothing, and with nothing he would leave it. How many useless efforts are invested in dedicating a whole life to fight and obtain that which not only cannot bring happiness to this life, but also has no use for life after death, for eternal life. And to think that there are so many people who foolishly squander this life that is as brief as a vapor that vanishes into thin air. This reminds us of the parable told by Jesus in Luke 12 about a rich man who devoted his life to amassing a great fortune. And when he thought he was going to live many years and was making plans to enjoy it he heard a voice announcing his end with these words, "You fool, this very night your life will be claimed from you. And who will keep what you have accumulated?"

Ecclesiastes 7:1 - 8:15

———

We come to chapter 7 of this Book of Ecclesiastes and here we find the last experiment performed by Solomon. As we said before, he made an experiment with his life and tried everything that could be done under the sun, looking for the possibility of obtaining satisfaction and enjoying his life, and he tried everything without finding that satisfaction. He tried science, he studied the natural laws of the universe, with which he was able to make some contribution, but it did not satisfy him at all. Then he turned to the study of philosophy and psychology. And it did not satisfy him either. He reached the limits of pleasure and materialism. He also tried fatalism, a rather popular philosophy of life today. And he tried selfish behavior, living for oneself. Then he tried religion; and no religion can satisfy because only Christ can satisfy the heart. Also riches was something that this man Solomon tried to enjoy. He was the richest man in the world. However, he found that his immense riches, by themselves, brought him no satisfaction.

Now we will see him try his last experiment: morality. The one who tries to find his satisfaction in morality would be considered a person who does good deeds for the benefit of others. And we would say that this is the direction in which most people are heading. That is the kind of person we are talking about in this section. So let's read the first verse of this chapter 7 of Ecclesiastes, which introduces us to Solomon

Seeking satisfaction in morality: the good life

"Better is good fame than good perfume, and better is the day of death than the day of birth."

By the way, this is true. There is nothing wrong with this statement: "Good reputation is better than good perfume". It is very nice for anyone to be able to hear people say that he is a good neighbor and has never given rise to conflicts or arguments. He gets along with everyone and does not argue about religion or politics, never takes a stand against another person and does not get into any kind of dubious or difficult situations. He limits himself to smiling and always adopts a middle line, without deviating from it to one side or the other. He is a respectable person, recognized in the community. He is a member of various organizations and is in contact with all kinds of people. And on the day of his death, the best that can be said of him will be said. Solomon said that this good reputation is something one should strive for here on earth. But will it bring satisfaction to the heart?

Verse 2, of this chapter 7, says:

"It is better to go to the house of mourning than to go to the house of feasting, for that is the end of all men, and he that liveth shall have it in his heart."

All this life of morality and good deeds is carried out in a dignified and decorous manner. The exemplary citizen, for example, attends a club to hear a lecture on environmental pollution. Since the talk does not compromise anyone's comfort or disrupt anyone's life, they will discuss the issue highlighting the seriousness of the problem, but none of those present will engage in practical action. On another occasion they will meet to talk about social problems but no one will personally engage in practical solutions. And all this without getting involved or showing any passion or enthusiasm for the serious problems being discussed. This could be an example of how things work in a community in a country where people live in relative prosperity.

That kind of life cannot satisfy a person's needs. It should not surprise us that young people have rebelled against such a conventional type of society, against such a comfortable way of being. Now, let's notice what verse 3 of this chapter 7 of Ecclesiastes says here:

"Better is sorrow than laughter, for with sadness of countenance the heart is mended."

People today, understandably, do everything possible to avoid affliction. The writer mentions here the heart as the seat of reflection and moral decisions and recommended people to reflect soberly on the brevity of life, rather than engage in foolish pleasures. Thus he went on to say in verse 4:

"The heart of the wise is in the house of mourning, but the heart of the foolish is in the house where joy reigns".

In other words, the wise man is mindful of death, but the foolish man thinks only of amusement. The foolish, when they see their friends departing from this life, do not think that they too are heading in the same direction. And their foolishness means that it does not occur to them to think what their final destiny will be. They do not consider it important to ask themselves if they are saved, or lost, or if they have a proper relationship with God. Let us continue reading verses 5 and 6:

"It is better to hear the rebuke of the wise than the song of fools, for the laughter of a fool is like the crackling of thorns under the pot. And this also is vanity."

Perhaps Solomon wondered, why not listen to both groups? Listen to the rebuke of the wise and then the laughter of the foolish. One group is better than the other, but it is easier to get along with both groups, to be popular with each. Some would not bear long listening to the rebuke of the wise. Let's see now, what verse 9 says:

"Be not hasty in your spirit to be angry, for anger rests in the bosom of fools."

Some people adopt a way of not getting angry for nothing. Being everyone's friend is a good formula for doing business with more people, without going to extremes and being willing to compromise, to compromise. By going with one group one day, and the next day with the other, you can become accepted by both.

Let us now read verse 11 of this seventh chapter of Ecclesiastes:

"Good is knowledge, or wisdom, with inheritance, and profitable to those who see the sun."

Here we have wisdom. We said at the beginning of our study of the Book of Proverbs, that wisdom is another name for Christ. God has made Christ our wisdom. Ah, how those who have adopted the way of good works to achieve satisfaction and enjoyment of life need Christ! And verse 12 goes on to say:

"For knowledge is a shield, and money is a shield; but wisdom is more advantageous, because it gives life to those who possess it."

There are those who consider money as a shield, as a protection, because they have it in abundance, but do not see the need to have Christ.

Here it says that "wisdom gives life to its possessors", we must always remember that life cannot be bought with money. Medical science may be able to extend your life by a few years, but it does not provide eternal life here nor beyond death, in eternity. Only wisdom, which is Christ, can give you that eternal life. Now, turning to verse 21, of this 7th chapter of Ecclesiastes, we read:

"Neither apply your heart to all things that are said, lest you hear your servant when he speaks evil of you."

Here you are advised not to be disturbed when news reaches you that someone who knows you well says you are a bad person. If you take a moderate, middle-of-the-road position, you will be applauded by the community in the long run.

seeking satisfaction in life simply by doing good deeds is tantamount to living like a vegetable, not like a human being. There are many young people who have rebelled against this comfortable spirit and against the hypocrisy of living one life during the week, and a different one, of appearances, on Sunday. And many are coming to have an encounter with Christ. In their youth, they have tried all that life has to offer and, in many cases, they have not found Christ in their homes, even though their parents professed a Christianity of forms, even though they attended church on Sunday. They realized that something important was missing in the environment in which they moved. They have seen firsthand the hypocrisy, the emptiness of life of those who pretend to be moralists, hiding behind their good works.

We believe it is easier to win an atheist than a hypocritical churchgoer. The atheist may respond when he hears the Gospel for the first time, but the one who attends church for convenience has already heard the Gospel over and over again and has become hardened, desensitized to the message of Christ. And that is a tragedy.

And now we come to the:

Chapter 8

This chapter continues to speak of the lukewarm man, who is not enthusiastic about anything. His character can be described as "neither hot nor cold". He says that he is living by the golden rule, but he does not seem to have any idea what the golden rule is or what it requires. Solomon observed that there did not seem to be much difference between the wicked and the righteous. Let us, then, highlight the salient points of this chapter. The first verse of Ecclesiastes chapter 8 reads:

"Who is like a wise man, like one who knows how to interpret things? The wisdom of man illuminates his face and changes the coarseness of his countenance".

Only Christ, who is true wisdom, can change a person's life. He can come into a life and bring excitement, joy and peace. He can provide us today with all the things necessary to free us from living a mediocre existence. Then the next 2 verses, verses 2 and 3 say:

"I counsel thee to keep the king's commandment, because of the oath which thou hast sworn before God. Do not hasten to depart from his presence, nor persist in any evil thing; for he will do whatever he pleases."

Solomon was saying, "Be careful what you do, don't get into trouble!" And verse 4, adds:

"For the king's word is sovereign, and no man shall say unto him, What doest thou?"

Now the king could take a stand for what he believed in because he had the freedom to do so. why not act like a king, with that freedom, and make the decision to come to Christ?

Once we asked a rebellious young man, whose appearance went against all conventionalism: "Why have you adopted a lifestyle like this? Why are you dressed like that?" And he answered: "Well, I want freedom, I want to be free. I want to live as I please. Then we asked him, "If you were to change the way you dress, and then go back to your group of friends, would they accept you?" He thought for a moment and replied, "I don't think they would accept me." Then we said, "So, you don't have much freedom, do you? You have to follow the rules that those people dictate to you."

And apparently so. Many young people believe they must have the approval of the gang, so they really don't know what freedom is. Many of them drink excessively or take drugs for no other reason than to be accepted by their circle. Another person also asked the aforementioned young man another question, "Look, do you think I don't have freedom because I dress this way?" "Well," said the young man, "yes, I would say that." Then the other person said, "Well, I have a freedom that you don't have at present. I don't have to dress this way all the time. I can dress the way I want to dress and I do. I don't have to submit to a mandatory model or style. So I have that freedom. And then the person of our acquaintance continued, "You and I are living in a world that is in rebellion against God; humanity is headed in that direction. But I can bow before the Lord Jesus Christ. I can call Him my Lord and my Savior. And this is true freedom. I do not follow the direction of the crowd, of the majority. I have made my own choice. If you want real freedom, not an imitation, come to Christ. He himself said in John 8:36, 36So if the Son sets you free, you will be free indeed." So much for the quote of the conversation. And that is genuine and eternal freedom. That is the freedom that you too can have.

Returning to our text, people find it difficult to understand that he who is striving to do good works to find satisfaction for his soul is in rebellion against God and as a prisoner in a jail, firmly bound to the rules or traditions of that lifestyle that his group or environment has set for him. And let's see what verse 8 of this chapter 8 of Ecclesiastes says here:

> *"There is no man that hath power over the breath of life, that he may preserve it, neither hath he power over the day of death. And no weapons are of any value in such a war, neither shall wickedness deliver the wicked."*

This is a solemn thought and a great warning. These words describe the pathetic helplessness of the human being in the face of the end of his own life. And verse 11, of this chapter 8, says:

"If the sentence to punish an evil deed is not executed at once, the hearts of the sons of men are disposed to do evil."

What a picture we have here of our contemporary society! When laws are not enforced, the wickedness of human beings evades the limits imposed by society, because evil resides in the human heart. Even some professing Christians believe that they can sin with impunity and that if God's punishment has not yet reached them, it will not come. But He is waiting for them somewhere along the way. That is why the following words of the apostle Paul in 2 Corinthians 6:2 are so timely: "Now is the accepted time; now is the day of salvation." Life is a gift and God gives you today to turn to Him.

Let us continue reading verse 14 of this eighth chapter of Ecclesiastes:

"There is vanity that is done upon the earth, for there are righteous to whom it happens as if they did the works of the wicked, and there are wicked to whom it happens as if they did the works of the righteous. I say that this also is vanity."

Solomon observed that when one looks at things superficially, there does not seem to be much difference between the wicked and the righteous. It seems to make no difference whether one is wicked or righteous, because they both end up the same way. And verse 15, says:

"Therefore, I praised joy, for man has no more good under the sun than to eat, drink, and be merry; and let this remain to him of his labor the days of his life which God grants him under the sun."

And this man ends by living this way: "let us eat and drink, for tomorrow we die". (As the phrase quoted in 1 Corinthians 15:32 says)

The conclusion is that the best one can do is to enjoy life and work in the days of life that God gives him in this world. that is the saddest, emptiest and most useless philosophy of life that anyone can have.

Ecclesiastes 9:1-14

In this section we have described the moralist as one who does good works. We have seen him as the person who believes that if he behaves well and acts honestly in all his affairs, God will accept him. He believes that he will go to heaven by the dynamics of his own efforts, because he is working for his salvation and furthermore, he considers himself a good person. He has a hard philosophy of life and very little true joy, which leads him to express some very sad and pessimistic conclusions.

We have seen that many of the teachings of Ecclesiastes are quite radical. They present the philosophy of the man who lives under the sun. They do not represent the point of view of the Christian, nor the point of view of God. They express to us the inevitable conclusions reached by that man under the sun, limited to the sphere of the earth. We consider this to be a sad book, and we especially notice it in this book. This book of the Bible is like a black sheep in a flock. One can find in this book many passages that seem to contradict others in the Holy Scriptures. They express ideas contrary to some of the great teachings of the Bible, which explains why this work has been a favorite among atheists. Volney and Voltaire often quoted it. It encourages a pessimistic philosophy of life, such as Schopenhauer had. Moreover, some cults or sects base the main theses of their systems on this book.

Now, how did this book come to be part of the canon of Scripture? Well, as with any other book, it is obvious that the author's purpose must be considered. What is his thesis? What is he trying to demonstrate? Is the writer trying to expound some Christian principles? We must always remember that Solomon was talking about a life apart from God. He was trying to conduct an experiment to see how human beings could be happy without God. And, here we have the conclusions he had reached as a human being living in this earthly sphere, under the sun, as he defined it. This is the perspective from which the human being contemplates life. So, it is not surprising that non-believers quote this book.

We would like to illustrate this as follows. Between high tide and low tide there is what is called "the mean tide", which is the sea level. Well, there is a way of life below sea level. And, there is also a way of life above sea level. So really, we have two different worlds. There's the world below sea level, and there are certain chemical elements there in a watery world. Above sea level there are different combinations of chemical elements in a world that is gaseous. Below sea level are fish with fins. Above sea level are birds with wings. They are two forms of life. The birds of the air don't tell the fish that something is wrong because they don't have feathers. Actually, the monkey and the barracuda fish might have some debate as to which way sea level is: for the barracuda fish, it's up. For the monkey, it's down.

Now, Ecclesiastes is under the sun. The Christian life is in the heavenly places, where God is. The man who lives under the sun will have a different point of view from the point of view of God who is "above the sun". So, now we are looking at two worlds, two different forms of life. Life under the sun is a worldly existence separated from God; it looks to a future and an eternity without God. Well, the Christian life stands in complete contrast to this earthly dimension, because in that life people have been saved by the grace of God and it constitutes a manifestation of divine grace.

So we have here two different spheres and the laws and principles of one cannot be applied to the other. They are as separate as that which is below sea level and that which exists above sea level. Since this is a reality, you may be wasting time by repeating to an unbeliever the words of the apostle Paul in Colossians 3:1 "If ye then be risen with Christ, seek those things which are above, where Christ sitteth on the right hand of God". That person listening to him is not even united with Christ; he is not spiritually risen with Christ. Consequently, he cannot seek the things that are above, the things of heaven. He must first be born again spiritually to become a new person. It is just not worth talking to someone who is not a Christian as if he were a person who is united to Christ, because he is not. It would be like trying to explain to a land tortoise how to fly. The land tortoise likes its natural environment, which is the earth, and is not even interested in flying.

Well, as we have seen, Ecclesiastes is the record of Solomon's experiments with life. He tried everything offered under the sun, to see if he could find satisfaction for his soul. All the teachings of this book must be interpreted in the light of this perspective.

Solomon tried the pursuit of knowledge and came to the conclusion in Ecclesiastes chapter 12 verse 22 that "much study is weariness to the body". He tried pleasure and the conclusion expressed in chapter 2 verse 17 was: "I abhorred life". He tried riches and came to the conclusion in chapter 5 verse 10, "He who loves money will not be satisfied with money". He then tried religion and concluded that it would make him a lunatic, an eccentric or a fanatic. Then he tried fame and good name; he tried practicing morality. And all he could say was that it was all vanity and affliction of spirit.

The writer Thackery wrote a fine novel called "The Vanity Fair". It is the story of a young girl named Becky, and it is set during the time of Napoleon's wars. It tells us about the pettiness and sinfulness of the lives of the characters, who lived their lives apart from God. The author was a Christian. And he concluded the book by saying, "The show is over, we put the puppets back in the box. All is vanity and affliction of spirit".

Incidentally, we can say that you could do the same in entertainment and amusement centers. There are capitals where fame and wealth are concentrated, where there is a real monopoly of tranquilizers and other drugs. And you will also come to the conclusion that life is empty without God and Christ.

It was Augustine who left us in his Confessions (book I, section 1) that oft-quoted expression: "You have made us for yourself, and the heart of man will remain restless until it rests in you. The human heart has been created in such a way that you could put the whole world inside it, and it would still not be full.

And so we have seen how Ecclesiastes has been used to support various ideologies, which do not provide answers to the problems of the human soul, Christ is the answer. The only answer. All other ways lead to emptiness and frustration. Only in the Lord Jesus Christ is life abundant.

Now, with all this in mind, let us examine this chapter 9, and read what the first verse says here:

"Surely I have given myself heartily to all these things, that I may declare that the righteous and the wise, and their works, are in the hand of God. And that men do not even know what is love or what is hate, though it is all before them."

That is, the writer was not concerned about the future. Eternity was a dimension he did not even think about because he knew nothing about it. And verse 2, he said:

"Everything happens in the same way to all; it is the same for the righteous and the wicked, the good, the pure and the impure, the one who sacrifices and the one who does not sacrifice, the good and the sinner, the one who swears and the one who is afraid to swear.

It seems to the writer that it doesn't matter in which direction one goes. For either way, the result will always be the same. Let us remember that this is not God's answer. This is the way the man who lives under the sun observes the lives of the people around him. And now let us read verse 3:

"This evil is among all that is done under the sun: that one and the same event befalls all, and that the hearts of the sons of men are full of evil and folly all their lives. And that after this they go with the dead."

So why work? Life would be like a big lottery and you would be a victim of circumstances. The person who has been lucky enough to win the prize should share it with you. The philosophies of our time are not saying anything new. Someone already tried to base a political ideology on this thinking and thought he had created a new system. But Solomon had already expressed it long before. Let us notice now, what verse 4 of this chapter 9 of Ecclesiastes says:

"There is still hope for everyone who is among the living, for better is a living dog than a dead lion."

If you follow this whole premise, the best option would then be: let us eat and drink, for tomorrow we die. Then it makes no difference whether you are wise or foolish. And yet it is better to be alive than dead, even if you live as a fool. As it says here, "it is better to be a living dog than a dead lion", Let us read, verse 5:

"For those who live know that they must die, but the dead know nothing, nor have they any more reward. Their memory falls into oblivion.

From here came this idea that the soul sleeps (and also from verse 10). Here we have the philosophy of the man under the sun, the earthly man. This is the conclusion reached if death is the end, and if there is nothing after death. It is for such a reason that he said that it was better a living dog than a dead lion.

God has told us what happens after death. The body is placed in the tomb, and it is the body that rests in that tomb. The Bible makes it clear that the soul of the child of God goes to be with the Lord. That is why the apostle Paul was able to write the following words in 2 Corinthians 5:6-8; "6So we live always with confidence, knowing that while we are in the body we are absent from the Lord 7(for we walk by faith, not by sight). 8But we are confident, and moreover we desire to be absent from the body and present to the Lord." The soul, the real person, is going to be with the Lord. As it says here, "absent from the body and present to the Lord." The bodies in which you and I are living are only our tents, our earthly abode, from which we will leave someday. So, as we have just seen, soul sleep is not even a Christian view.

Now, verse 6, of this 9th chapter of Ecclesiastes, says:

"Also their love, their hatred, and their envy perish; and they shall have no more part in all that is done under the sun."

In the beginning we already said that this was a sad chapter. It considers life as vain, empty, purposeless and meaningless. If death is the end of all things, then the human being is simply like an animal. An evolutionist would say that man was once, in the past, an animal. And this earthly man living under the sun says that man is like an animal now. The end result of both is the same. Man dies like an animal.

How different it is for us to know that we come from the creative hand of God, and that we are going back to Him! Now, verse 7, says:

"Go, eat your bread with joy and drink your wine with a glad heart, for your works are already pleasing to God."

The person who rules his life by the principle of good works, thinking that death is the end of all things, finds momentary satisfaction in pleasures such as food and drink. But he ends up realizing that his life is a monotonous succession without motivation or purpose. And verse 8 says:

"May your clothes be white at all times, and may your head never lack perfume.

For the one who is centered on this earth it is important to keep a good appearance of distinction before others. And verse 9, says:

"Enjoy life with the woman you love, all the days of the vain life that are given you under the sun, all the days of your vanity. This is your reward in life, and in the toil with which you toil under the sun."

The writer advised enjoying marriage. There are many marriages of non-Christians who are enjoying their life together. Of course, they go through their problems and their dark days, but their attitude is to face their life as best they can.

Now we come to another verse on which some base their theory of soul sleep. Let us read verse 10:

"Whatsoever thy hand findeth to do, do it according to thy strength: for in the grave, whither thou goest, there is no work, nor toil, nor knowledge, nor wisdom."

Of course it is, because when you put this body in the grave, this body that today can move to work, or use its brain to study or perform certain mental activities, when you put it in the grave, it will not be able to perform any kind of activity. Solomon was speaking only of the body, when he said "whatever comes to your hand to do, do it according to your strength". He was speaking of the hand, not the soul. And it is the hand that will be placed in the grave. If you are a child of God, you will go into the presence of the Lord. If you are not a child of God, you will go to the abode of the dead until you are resurrected to be judged.

So everything does not end with this life. It is evident that this book does not teach soul sleep.

We come now to verse 11, which talks about social injustice and minority groups. Let's listen to what verse 11 of this chapter 9 of Ecclesiastes says:

"I turned, and saw under the sun that neither to the swift is the race, nor war to the strong, nor yet bread to the wise, nor yet riches to the prudent, nor yet favor to the eloquent; for to all comes the time and the occasion."

The observations of the earthly man under the sun lead him to believe that this life is a matter of time and chance. It is nothing but a great lottery. And if you happen to be born into one race, you will have some problems; if you happen to be born into another, you will have other problems. Everything is left to chance and you can't do anything about it. This is the predominant thought here. Let us continue reading verse 12:

"Now neither doth man know his time: as the fish that are taken in the evil net, or as the birds that are snared in the snare, so are the sons of men caught in the evil time, when it falleth suddenly upon them."

If time and chance are the regulating factors of life, then you are as helpless as the fish caught in a net. And there is nothing you can do to change that fate. This is a terrible point of view, and the worst kind of fatalism. For the one who lives only to do good deeds in this life, there is no other explanation and he is bound to come to this fatalistic philosophy.

Now Solomon presented a little parable. Let us read verse 14:

"There was a small city, with few inhabitants, and there came a great king who laid siege to it and erected against it great bulwarks."

Listen carefully, because here is a parable. Are you sensitive to the plight of the oppressed, minority groups and the despised? You should be aware of the failure of human resources to eradicate poverty, abuse and discrimination. As many times in the past and throughout history, a powerful king appears in this story. It will not be the last time this happens and on this occasion, the inhabitants of the city became prisoners, unable to avoid the great deployment of forces that besieged them. This parable seems representative of all history, which has been characterized by wars, abuses of power, injustice and oppression. How much more time do you think God should give man to try to put an end to abuses of power, injustice and oppression?

Ecclesiastes 9:14 - 10:10

We are going to finish chapter 9 of this Book of Ecclesiastes, and surely you agree with us that this is a pessimistic chapter. It presents us with the point of view of the earthly man, who lives under the sun. It is the wrong conclusions that this man has reached and his pseudo-philosophy is due to his ignorance, his prejudices and his false premises based on his situation under the sun, apart from God.

We have seen his conclusion, and this is that all human beings will arrive at the same place. By this we must say that there are many things that this man sees that are obvious, but the conclusions he reaches are wrong. Next, we saw that death provides total integration and that all are equal in death. That is, that death is the great leveling process, and that is true.

As we read verse 12 we commented that if time and chance are the regulating factors of life, then you are as helpless as the fish caught in a net. And there is nothing you can do to change that fate. This is a terrible point of view, and the worst kind of fatalism. For the one who lives only to do good deeds in this life, there is no other explanation and he is bound to come to this fatalistic philosophy.

Now Solomon presented a little parable. Let us read verse 14:

"There was a small city, with few inhabitants, and there came a great king who laid siege to it and erected against it great bulwarks."

Listen carefully, because here is a parable. Are you sensitive to the plight of the oppressed, minority groups and the despised? You should be aware of the failure of human resources to eradicate poverty, abuse and discrimination. As many times in the past and throughout history, a powerful king appears in this story. It will not be the last time this happens and on this occasion, the inhabitants of the city became prisoners, unable to avoid the great deployment of forces of those who besieged them. This parable seems representative of all history, which has been characterized by wars, abuses of power, injustice and oppression. How much more time do you think God should give man to try to put an end to abuses of power, injustice and oppression?

Now in verse 15, of this 9th chapter of Ecclesiastes, we read:

"But there was a poor and wise man in it, who delivered the city by his wisdom, and no one remembered that poor man!"

And who was that man who came and delivered that city? His name was wisdom; and wisdom is another name for Christ, for in First Corinthians chapter 1 and verse 30 we read that God has made Christ our wisdom. And Christ came to this earth in poverty. That is why He could say in Matthew 8:20: "Foxes have holes, and the birds of the air have nests, but the Son of Man has nowhere to lay His head". On this earth Christ was therefore a poor man. Now, turning to verses 16 and 17, of this 9th chapter of Ecclesiastes, we read:

"Then I said, 'Wisdom is better than strength, though the knowledge of the poor is despised and his words are not heard. The quiet words of the wise are better than the cry of the lord among fools."

Finally, the voice of the Lord Jesus Christ will prevail. When He comes, His voice will be like the shout of an archangel and like the sound of a trumpet (1 Thessalonians 4:16) Today a great murmur of voices may be heard in this world, but there will come a day when His voice will prevail on this earth over all others. Now, verse 18, of this 9th chapter of Ecclesiastes, says:

"Better is wisdom than weapons of war; but a single error destroys much good."

And here we have the conclusion of this chapter 9 and that is that wisdom is better than weapons of war. And Christ, it is superior to nuclear energy.

Now, it says here, "Wisdom is better than weapons of war". And that is true in today's world. You have been able to observe the great ocean liners today, which travel great distances on the seas without having the route marked on the water and with all ease, the pilots and their great vessels are able to take those ships and their passengers to their respective destinations. And how can they do that? Well, they do it by following the wise principles that were laid down by a little known Greek philosopher many years ago, who conducted research in geometry. Truly, better is wisdom than weapons of war.

And then, comes the phrase "but a single error destroys much good". Another version translates: "but a single sinner destroys much good". The life of an individual can exert a lot of influence. And the influence is always stronger when it is used in the wrong direction. History has confirmed this reality.

Well, we can look at history. Adam's sin has affected the entire human race. During the conquest of Canaan, Achan sinned and consequently, a whole nation suffered a defeat. And they had to deal with Achan's sin before they could achieve a victory. King Rehoboam divided the kingdom of Israel. Centuries later, in the times of the church in the New Testament, the sin of Ananias and Sapphira produced the first serious incident to the early church and from those days on, the church would no longer act as powerfully as it did at the beginning.

You and I, we have a certain amount of influence, either for good or for evil. No matter who you are, you occupy a place of influence. As the apostle Paul said in Romans chapter 14 verse 7, none of us lives to himself, neither do we die to ourselves. It is as if you are a preacher, a propagator of an idea. No one can avoid being a communicator of something and by the kind of life they live they exert an influence on others.

We believe that the one who performs good works and boasts of his moral life apart from God is a great obstacle to others. It is as if he blocks others from the way to God because his message is: "Live as I live, without God. I simply do good works". This message thus constitutes a hindrance, creating confusion in others.

And you, no matter where you are or who you are, you are also a communicator. You are transmitting with your life some message to those around you in the wide circle of human society. You can influence your neighborhood, your immediate community. You can be of influence to other Christians in your church, who are watching you to see if you are serious about your relationship with God and your relationship with the church. And in the smallest of circles, which is the family, you are affecting other people's lives.

Recall that the apostle Peter preached an eloquent message on the day of Pentecost. Andrew was there listening to him and must have been able to say: "This is my brother. I introduced him to Christ. And that was Andrew's influence. You, by your words and actions, by your life, are pointing others to heaven or to hell. Now, if you want to go to hell, that's up to you. But you have no right to lead a child, your family, or other people close to you there. It is terrible to lead others that way! We have influence over others, and that is a great responsibility. Let's think about it.

We now move on and arrive at the:

Chapter 10

We can see here that the injustices of life suggest the adoption of a moderate way of living. Let us listen to what the first verse of this chapter 10 says here:

"Dead flies make a bad smell and corrupt the perfume of the perfumer; so is a little folly to him who is esteemed wise and honorable."

Life offers us a complete illustration of this truth. A night out on the town may cause you to live in darkness all your life, endure illness and even face death. We know of several real-life examples of such experiences; several people have told us of their bitterness at not being able to rectify a mistake, a single action that ruined the rest of their lives.

We know of many cases of parents who have spent years busy training their child and supporting him in his studies, only to have a harmful friendship appear, a young man or woman, who drags him or her into an action that totally deviates him or her from his or her career, from his or her goals and transforms him or her into a failed person. And so, a small folly, a small display of foolishness was all it took to spoil, to ruin the life of a normally wise and sensible person, and to seriously affect the lives of those closest to him. listen to these words of this first verse expressed by another version: "Dead flies stink and spoil good perfume. A little foolishness weighs more than wisdom and honor put together". This is indeed, a tragic reality.

Now, the second verse of this chapter 10, says:

"The heart of the wise man is at his right hand, but the heart of the fool at his left hand."

The right hand is the hand that represents strength. That is why it says that the heart of the sage guides him to the right hand. Whatever he does, he does with all his heart. He does not do it reluctantly, grudgingly. And the heart of the fool guides him to his left hand. He does things without enthusiasm, without interest.

How does this illustration apply to life? Whatever you do in life, do it from the heart. If you are going to serve God, do it not with reluctance, but with joy and excitement. Do not make the Christian life something painful and sad. Make it something really worthwhile. Whatever you do, do it with enthusiasm. And verse 3, it says:

"Even as he goes on his way, the fool lacks sanity, and goes about telling everyone that he is a fool."

A fool does not need to wear a sign identifying him as a fool. The truth is that all he has to do is open his mouth. And sometimes he doesn't even have to open his mouth to prove that he is a fool. So the Bible calls him a fool, and he confirms to everyone that, indeed, he is. Now, verse 4, it says:

"Though the ruler's spirit be exalted against you, do not lose your temper, for meekness makes great offenses cease."

That is, if you cannot fight them, unite your forces with those of your rivals. That is exactly what the earthly man thinks, the one who lives and thinks under the sun.

Let us now note what verses 5 and 6 of this chapter 10 of Ecclesiastes say:

"There is an evil that I have seen under the sun, by way of error emanating from the ruler: that foolishness is placed in many high places, while the rich sit in humble places."

And this is one of the things that happens in our time. Sin has been given a dignity. There was a time when sin was something despicable that was only found in certain areas of the city. It was considered something dirty, obscene, uncouth. It had the image of something low, lowly. But today, sin has moved to the better parts of the city. And it is committed with great dignity. It has been given a very important place. And it occupies a very prominent place in some television programs, in which some of the interviewees even exhibit it as a sign of distinction, as a sign that they move in high-level environments. And if on top of that they show an eccentric or uncontrolled, or aggressive personality, they provoke a current of sympathy in their favor.

On the other hand, interviews granted to ordinary citizens, to Christians, are not profitable for that media, because they have a very low audience. And yet, they are the ones who are making the best contribution to the welfare of their community and society in general. And so, they occupy a lower place in people's preferences. That is why and as another version of this verse 6 puts it, "the foolish are given many high places, but the able are given the lowest places". Let us now listen to what it says now, verse 7, of this chapter 10 of Ecclesiastes:

"I have seen servants on horses, and princes walking as servants upon the earth."

Working hard, saving your money, and studying hard, late into the night, does not always mean that one day you will become successful. Maybe the foolish or lazy person who lives next door to you will inherit millions. And that is often the case today. Sometimes those who face the struggle of life with the least effort, or by taking advantage of the efforts of others, are the ones who occupy the highest positions in society. That is the image that this verse leaves us with.

We also know outstanding Christians, who have a humble character. Some live in modest homes and others are well-to-do. However, as they lead normal lives, they are not noted for their popularity. They are, as verse 7 says, "princes walking as servants upon the earth."

Let us continue reading the following verse, verse 8 of the tenth chapter of Ecclesiastes:

"Whosoever diggeth a pit shall fall into it; and whosoever breaketh through a wall, the serpent shall bite him."

It would be foolish for you to believe that you can sin and get away with it and avoid the consequences, especially if you are a child of God. God may not act immediately, but all you need to do is wait, and He will eventually judge you for it. Over the years we have seen it happen this way. We have observed believers who have made serious mistakes, and have never been able to escape the consequences. At some point in their lives God begins to act, and disciplines them as a father disciplines his children. Now, let's notice what verse 9 says here:

"He who cuts stones, is wounded by them; he who splits wood, in it he is endangered."

The one who cut or removed stones in those days was removing the signs that demarcated the properties. Here again it is being stated that one cannot avoid the consequences of sin. As the apostle Paul told the Galatians in 6:7, "whatsoever a man sows, that shall he also reap". If someone tries to cheat someone out of what rightfully belongs to him, or tries to abuse in some other way, God will see to it that the abuser gets paid. That is why the Lord Jesus Christ told us, in Romans 12:19: "Avenge not yourselves, my beloved, but rather give place unto the wrath of God: for it is written, Vengeance is mine, I will repay, saith the Lord". He will settle accounts with the offender and set things right. Then, verse 10, says:

"If the iron is dull and its edge is not ground, the effort must be increased; it is profitable to use wisdom".

If the hoe with which you work loses its edge, if you know your profession well, you will sharpen it, because if not, it will be much more difficult to try to work digging in the earth with it. And unfortunately, and figuratively speaking, how many people today are not willing to do what is necessary to sharpen the hoe. Today, even in the Christian life, many want to throw themselves into serving God without taking into account the importance of a good personal preparation. The advice here is to prepare the tools of the trade well. No one should expect to cut many weeds with a blunt hoe. First it is necessary to sharpen it and only then to go out on the road to cut the weeds effectively. It is evident that this book of Ecclesiastes contains great lessons for practical living that we would do well to apply. It is truly a book out of the ordinary.

Ecclesiastes 10:11 - 11:10

———

Let us return today to chapter 10 of this Book of Ecclesiastes that we are studying and let us consider what is said here from verse 11 onwards. Let us remind you that we are still in this section that we call "seeking satisfaction in morality". That is, the life characterized by good works. This was a quest an experiment that Solomon was conducting. This was the last experiment he made, and, probably, he spent more time on this one than on any of the others he made. The longer section deals with this particular period.

Let us begin our reading with verse 11 of this chapter 10 of Ecclesiastes:

"If the snake bites before it is charmed, the charmer is of no use."

It is necessary that we understand the customs of the east if we are to understand what this verse is telling us. It is very similar to the Biblical passage found in the Book of Psalms 58:4 and 5. There King David presented us with a reference to snakes, and the way they act and said: "They have venom like the venom of a serpent; they are like a deaf viper that shuts his ear, that hears not the voice of them that charms, no matter how skilful the charmer may be". In another passage we also have the same idea. It is Jeremiah 8:17, which says: "I will send serpents upon you, vipers against which there is no enchantment, and they shall bite you, saith the Lord."

The viper is a reptile, a snake that has a deadly venom, as we already know. Surely you have seen one of those Indian fakirs, a person sitting on the ground with a small flute playing a sad little melody to charm a cobra that is in a wicker basket. The snake makes undulating movements following the sound of the flute. The cobra will not attack as long as the sound of the flute remains. But there are times when the snake does not listen, and then it may strike; and when it does, it can be deadly.

In the passages we have mentioned, we do not believe that the writers are referring to serpents in a literal way. We think they are referring to those people we call charlatans, who can deceive you, who can betray you. For example, people like Judas Iscariot, the one who betrayed Jesus. After all, that is what according to the Bible the Antichrist will do to the nation of Israel in the great tribulation period.

Even among Christians you will find people who speak and should not speak, because they say things that are not true. That is why Solomon said in this verse 11, "If the serpent bites before he is charmed, the charmer is of no avail". That person may pretend to be your friend, but he will bite you like a snake, even if you have been good to him.

That was the kind of grief David felt when his friend Ahithophel turned against him. Ahithophel had been his counselor and personal friend, but he abandoned David and went with Absalom when Absalom rebelled against his father David. That experience broke David's heart. We believe that David was a broken man after Absalom's rebellion. Up to that time, when David was at his peak, we doubt that there was ever a king like David. After that betrayal and rebellion, David became an old man and in Psalm 55 poured out the sorrow of his heart. This is the image of this verse 11.

Solomon was saying that, in the possibility of this happening, one should be very careful. We could say that this is the philosophy of life in an ordinary person of our time. He is the person who does good deeds as long as it does not compromise him with anyone, nor does it cause him any trouble. Surely he will have been told to be careful with such and such a person because he can repeat what he said and change it, twist it. So when you meet such people, you will be very kind to them, but you will be very careful what you say to them.

Sometimes it seems that we should really confront that kind of person who takes the facts and distorts them, pointing out to him exactly what he is doing. However, from experience we have seen that if you confront certain people, you will be aggressively attacked. Let us now note what verse 12 of this chapter 10 says:

"The words of the wise are full of grace, but the lips of the foolish cause their own ruin."

It is well said here that "the lips of a fool cause his own ruin", and it should be added that also those around him. It is for this reason that we should be careful in making friends and choose quality friends.

There are some professors at colleges and universities who caution new students by telling them: "You will make new friends here and some of them will last a lifetime. Some of you may even find your future wife or husband here (and in some cases you will), but you should be careful about the friends you choose.

Also when our children begin to study it is good to give them advice like this. Telling them that they have a great opportunity to get excellent friends, but that they should be careful because some of them can end up spoiling their lives.

Some people are like asps or snakes. If one is kind to them and can arouse their sympathy, things will go well. But you have to be cautious in the way you act in front of them. This is good advice for the person who wants to be diplomatic, and who likes to keep the middle ground so as not to get into trouble. Now, in verses 13 and 14 of this chapter 10, we read:

"The beginning of the words of his mouth is foolishness; the end of his talk, noxious raving. A fool multiplies his words. If no one knows what is to come to pass, who will let him know what will be after him?"

This is true and it happens in reality. You have probably noticed that usually when you get together with a group to discuss some topic, there is always one person who is especially loquacious. Sometimes that person monopolizes the entire conversation and will say inane or absurd things. And immediately the group begins to wish that person would shut up, and it is often difficult to get him or her to stop talking and interrupting others. To avoid this, some lecturers, when they reach the colloquium period, ask those present to write down their questions and send them to them. This seems to be the only way to avoid the emergence of an excessively loquacious person who only seeks to highlight his or her own prominence or introduce problems. Someone has said that there are people whose brains transmit to the mouth the order to speak, and then the brain stops working while the mouth continues to emit sounds.

Let's go ahead now and read what verse 15 says:

"Fools are so much fatigued by work that they do not even know which way to go to the city."

This is a proverbial expression that indicates extreme ignorance, just like another contemporary expression that there are people who would not even know how to get out of the rain. Then, verse 16, says:

"Woe unto thee, O land, when thy king is a boy, and thy princes feast from the morning!"

Here he is talking about those who give themselves completely to pleasure instead of ruling their people properly, so that they are not a blessing to their people. Then he says in verse 17:

"Blessed art thou, O land, when thy king is the son of nobles, and thy princes eat at their hour to replenish their strength and not to drink!"

We would say that one of the main problems in most nations today is not drugs, but drinking. We are talking about alcohol. There are millions of alcoholics today. In many countries alcoholism causes social alarm. The health authorities warn about the destructive effects that an alcoholic suffers in his organism and the traffic authorities have notably hardened the legislation and the control on the drivers, due to the high number of accidents caused by people who drive under the effects of the drink. An alarming factor is also the fact that young people begin to drink alcohol without control even before they reach adolescence. In this verse we see the contrast with the previous verse, because here the rulers give their people an example of work, total dedication and sobriety. Now, verse 18, of this chapter 10 of Ecclesiastes, tells us:

"Because of laziness the roof falls down, and because of idleness there are leaks in the house".

Here we have a severe criticism against laziness, against refusing the most elementary and indispensable jobs in the sphere of the home. Sometimes when people greet each other with phrases like "have a nice day" or "take it easy" what they want to wish the other person is that he has to work as little as possible and that he enjoys himself, that he has the best time he can. Now, verse 19, says:

"For pleasure the feast is made, wine gladdens the living, and money answers for everything."

Another version translates this verse thus: "To rejoice, bread; to rejoice, wine; to enjoy, money." Some people who have great financial resources think that money can satisfy all their desires. Let us now continue with verse 20, which reads:

"Neither speak thou evil of the king in thy mind, nor in the secret of thy chamber speak evil of the rich man: for the fowls of the air shall carry the voice, the winged creatures shall tell him."

This verse tells us "Do not even in your thoughts speak evil of the king". The ruler, by reason of his office, deserves respect and should not be ridiculed. In the New Testament the apostle Peter said in his first letter, chapter 2, verse 17, "Honor the king." And, of course, the same applies to those who lead a nation under other forms of government.

We now come to the:

Chapter 11

Of this Book of Ecclesiastes and here we find the best course of action to be followed by those who base their relationship with God on the practice of good works, for those who proclaim to live according to their moral principles, who do not want to commit themselves to anything, but rather adopt an intermediate, neutral position. From a spiritual point of view, they are neither hot nor cold. In verse 1, of this chapter 11, we read:

"Cast thy bread upon the waters; after many days thou shalt find it."

This is an invitation to perform good deeds. Even if the reward is slow in coming, those actions will not go unrewarded. Then, in verse 2 we read:

"Deal to seven, and even to eight, for thou knowest not what evil shall come upon the earth."

In other words, when you are doing good, try to help more than one person. Try to help several, because maybe you will have problems in the future and, then, many people will be willing to help you.

Let us remember that the Lord Jesus Christ presented a parable dealing with this very subject, which was recorded in Luke 16. On that occasion he spoke of an "unjust" steward who, in reality, stole. He won friends for himself by lowering their debt to their master, so that when he was out of work, he could go to them for help. Now, in verse 3, we read:

"If the clouds are full of water, they shall pour it out upon the earth; and if the tree falls toward the south, or toward the north, in the place where the tree falls, there it shall remain."

If rain is forecast, take it seriously and be prepared. After a big tree falls, it is difficult to move it from its place. What is being said here? That it is better to have a clear idea and understanding of a situation at the very beginning of it, before launching into an enterprise because, after you start, it is very difficult to make changes. Now, in verse 4, we read:

"He that regardeth the wind shall not sow, and he that regardeth the clouds shall not reap."

This is advice to act wisely in everything one does. If someone wants to sow seed, he had better wait until there is no wind to scatter the seed. If someone wants to reap a harvest, he will not start if there is threat of rain. Moving on, verse 5, says:

"Just as you do not know the way of the wind or how the bones grow in the womb of a woman with child, so you do not know the work of God, who makes all things."

The formation of the fetus and the physical birth of a child are still great mysteries today. And spiritual birth is an even greater mystery. We do not know how the Holy Spirit works. In John 3:8 the Lord Jesus said: "8 The wind blows where it wills, and you hear the sound of it, but you do not know where it comes from or where it goes. So is everyone who is born of the Spirit". Admittedly, we are ignorant of many things.

In view of these limitations the teaching here is the following: "Do not let what you do not know cause you problems as to what you do know". Although on the one hand we recognize that God has allowed some details of the Bible to remain a mystery, because our mind is limited to understand the totality of the plans and purposes in history, on the other hand, there is much that He has clearly revealed to us and that not only concerns salvation, eternal life, but also encompasses the main aspects of God's Will for our life as Christians. So we must not let what we do not know alter or impair what we do know. Now, let us read in verses 7 and 8 of Ecclesiastes 11:

> *"Soft indeed is the light and pleasant to the eyes to see the sun; but though a man may live many years and in all of them have joy, let him remember that the days of darkness will be many, and that whatever comes is vanity."*

In other words, you will be old someday. And life in old age will not always be pleasant and enjoyable. Finally for today, let's read verses 9 and 10:

> *"Rejoice, young man, in your youth, and let your heart take pleasure in the days of your adolescence. Walk according to the promptings of your heart and the taste of your eyes, but remember that in all these things God will judge you. Therefore put away wrath from your heart and put away evil from your body, for youth and youth are vanity".*

Remember, if you are young, now is the time to make your decisions in all categories of life, and it is important that you make the right decisions in these years. And it is important that you make the right decisions in these years. How many have wasted, wasted their lives and are living wasted lives today, because of the wrong decisions of their youth!

The days of youth are empty if they are not lived in the most appropriate way. Life is a gift that God has given us, one day at a time; in fact, one second at a time. It is a beautiful gift, and it is to be used for the honor and glory of God. What is the main purpose of the human being? The main purpose is to honor, glorify God and enjoy Him forever.

We suggest that you read chapter 12, the last chapter of Ecclesiastes, to familiarize yourself with its contents and thus be better prepared.

Ecclesiastes 12

We come to chapter 12 of this Book of Ecclesiastes which presents us with a pessimistic view of life. We have seen that Solomon had made an experiment in life. He was probably the only man who has ever lived who, because of his great financial resources, was able to conduct an experiment in all these different areas of life. He tried to find a solution and satisfaction to life apart from God. The key expression that we find repeated over and over again in this Book is that of under the sun. In his first experiment, Solomon tried to find the solution in nature, what we would call today, the natural sciences.

There are a lot of people who think that if you go back to nature you can find the solution to your problems. Today there is a great exodus of people leaving the urban center of the city to the suburbs and even further, to the countryside or the mountains, places where they buy or rent an apartment or house. The purpose is to escape the noise, pollution or the burden of large urban concentrations. Now, this did not solve Solomon's problems, nor will it solve ours. So Solomon tried philosophy and wisdom; pleasure, materialism, that is, trying to live for the "now", and then fatalism. And he tried to live for himself, that is, he tried selfishness. Later he tried religion and found ritual, but without a spiritual reality. Then he tried to find the answer in riches, but greed makes the human heart insatiable. It is never satisfied. Then Solomon tried to lead the life of the moralist, but he found that it was an insipid existence. This is the reason why many young people have rebelled against that kind of life.

And now we come to the last conclusion reached by Solomon. The last paragraph can be titled:

A poetic figure of old age

This chapter includes something for the young and for the elderly. So in this chapter we will find those two extreme stages of life. Let's read then verse 1 of this chapter 12 of Ecclesiastes.

"Remember thy Creator in the days of thy youth, before the evil days come, and the years come, of which thou shalt say, I have no pleasure in them."

In light of the fact that nothing under the sun can satisfy the human heart, Solomon said, "Turn to God." Solomon was exhorting the young men in their youth to make a decision to draw near to God. As the story continues, the motives for making that decision become clear.

Solomon was going to paint a picture of old age, a picture that would not be very attractive. However, it is a real picture of human beings in old age. Perhaps young people reading it will wonder if that stage of their lives will actually be like that. But then, when they reach a certain age, they will have to recognize that this description of old age is accurate.

Some skeptics say, "I believe in a religion for here and now. I am not interested in a religion of the hereafter." Well, here in these pages we have a religion for the here and now, for this present life, which involves being properly related to God and living for Him. Why? Well, let's look at the picture that Solomon painted of the old age, a picture that he painted very realistically. Well, let's listen to what he said here in verse 2 of this 12th chapter of Ecclesiastes:

"Before the sun and the light, the moon and the stars are darkened, and the clouds return after the rain."

Does it mean that the stars shining in the heavens will fade away? No, it means that your eyesight will not be as good as it was when you were young. And you will have to resort to reading glasses.

And time goes by, and bad experiences follow one after another. And it says here: "And let the clouds return after the rain". A person can go out and have a lot of fun, but then he has to dedicate two, or three or four days to rest because the human body needs more time for physical recovery. Then verse 3 tells us:

"When the guards of the house tremble, and the strong men stoop; when those who grind cease to work, for they will have diminished, and those who look out of the windows are left in darkness."

Here we have a description of the body, of the physical body in old age. What, then, are those keepers of the house? We think he is referring to the legs. The elderly person loses firmness and has a tendency to stagger.

You may have noticed an elderly person who has to be helped to get on and off a bus or out of a car. Even if your friends tell you that you are in good health, there is always someone who tries to help you with one of these tasks. Because the elderly person is not as agile and quick as he or she used to be.

People of this age, when they begin to descend stairs, sometimes groan. This reminds us of what the apostle Paul wrote in 2 Corinthians 5:4, "We who are in this tent groan with anguish." (another version says "sighing and being burdened.") It is because their legs do not respond as they used to. (another version says "sighing and being burdened.") It is that their legs no longer respond to them as they used to. Trying to go up and down stairs begins to be a nuisance and pains appear in the knees. Soon the need for the help of a cane becomes apparent.

What a picture, then, we have here before us, my friend reader! And Solomon went on to describe a body in a state of general decay. Then he said, "and let the strong men stoop." Here he was referring to the shoulders, which can no longer stand erect as before, in the time of youth and maturity, and begin to stoop, adopting a posture which, under these conditions, is more comfortable for the body.

And then he continues this description with the phrase: "when those that grind cease to work, because they will have diminished". Those that grind are the teeth. Here we are referring to the loss of teeth and the person becomes more dependent on the dentist to prevent or cope with natural wear and tear, to replace teeth, to place bridges or dentures.

And the description of this verse is completed with the phrase "and they that look out of the windows shall be darkened". Here it refers to the progressive loss of sight. So these windows of the body begin to darken. Things no longer look as bright as they did before. Then, in verse 4, of this 12th chapter of Ecclesiastes, it says:

"When the doors outside close, and the noise of the mill dies away; when the voice of the bird is heard, but the songs cease to be heard."

The first phrase "when the outer doors close" is almost a poetic description referring to the loss of the sense of hearing.

We continue reading in the same verse 4: "when the voice of the bird is heard". Young people are not even awakened in the morning by the alarm clock. Neither do they mind the noise children make, and they like to listen to music at maximum volume. However, for older people, any bird singing at dawn can wake them up.

Then he tells us at the end of verse 4 "but the songs cease to be heard". Evidently older people can no longer sing the way they used to. Even singers, those who once had magnificent voices, are losing the quality and power of their voices.

And so Solomon continued to talk about old age. And then he came to a point that we consider tragic, because now we are going to observe the psychological effects. Let us now read verse 5:

"When the heights also shall be feared, and the way shall be full of dangers, and the almond tree shall flourish, and the locust shall be a burden, and the caper shall lose its effect; for man goes to his eternal abode, and mourners shall prowl the streets."

It says here in the first sentence "when one is also afraid of heights". In other words, the elderly no longer like to travel as they did when they were young. And small things worry them, things that in other times did not bother them, considering them insignificant.

Then the writer said, "And let the road be filled with dangers." Things are no longer enjoyed as they were in the past. There are old people who loved to travel and travel long distances, all over the world. When they were young, they were not so concerned about the way they traveled, the condition of the vehicles, or the mode of transportation used. They liked the adventure of unpredictability, new situations, improvisation and change of plans. But as the years go by, things change and then they worry about details that did not worry them before and, in any case, they feel insecure or fear any alteration of the planned plan, or any situation that could represent a danger.

Then, we are told here following with this verse 5, "and let the almond tree blossom". When the almond tree blossoms, it shows white blossoms. And that means that the person who is close to old age will see that his head will be full of gray hair, his hair will turn gray, then white. Or else, perhaps they will be completely lost due to the effects of baldness.

Now, let's notice what Solomon goes on to say here, in this same verse 5, "and let the locust be a burden." How can a small locust become a burden? It is that when old age comes, small deeds or details that never bothered us, become a burden. Take grandchildren, for example. If you are already an old man and you have grandchildren, of course you love them and like to spend some time with them; but after a few hours, you breathe a sigh of relief when your parents take them away, don't you? Because strength fails, endurance capacity is no longer the same, and patience is more quickly exhausted. Then even small things become a burden.

Then we are told here in this same verse 5: "and the caper loses its effect". What happens is that the old man's organism is so weakened that the stimulating properties of this plant called caper no longer have any effect. In addition, there is a loss of appetite.

And finally this verse 5 says, "for man goes to his eternal abode, and mourners will prowl the streets". As death approaches, the human being is close to eternity. Let us continue the description by reading verse 6 of Ecclesiastes 12:

"Before the silver chain breaks, the gold bowl breaks, the pitcher breaks by the fountain, and the pulley or wheel breaks over the well."

In this verse we have a list of organs of the body. Towards the end of life, they begin to stop functioning or function defectively. That "silver chain" is the spinal cord. That "golden bowl" is the head, the cavity or receptacle for the brain. The functioning of the brain decreases in efficiency with increasing age, and at the time of death it ceases to function completely.

"The pitcher that breaks by the fountain" refers to the lungs. "The pulley or wheel that breaks over the well" is the heart. Blood is no longer pumped through the body. This whole description is a picture of the deterioration of old age that eventually leads to death. Life cannot be sustained without the functioning of these organs.

Then, in verse 7, the writer said:

"Before the dust returns to the earth, as it was, and the spirit returns to God who gave it."

The soul does not sleep. And we would like those people who use verses from the book of Ecclesiastes to support their ideas about the sleep of the soul to just keep reading until they come to this verse. The body rests, but the spirit, or soul, returns to God, who gave it.

We reiterate that the New Testament assures us that to be absent from the body means to be present with the Lord (as we see in 2 Corinthians 5:8). The soul returns immediately to God. The body is simply a tabernacle, a tent in which we live. It is like an outer shell. The soul goes to be with God.

Then, in verse 8, of this 12th chapter of Ecclesiastes, we read:

"Vanity of vanities, said the Preacher, all is vanity!"

Life is a real void if you are living it for nothing but here and now. Someday you will discover that all you have in your hand is nothing but a handful of ashes, and that before you lies a whole eternity. One writer put it this way: "When I was a child I laughed and cried, and time crawled; when I was young I dreamed and talked, and time walked; when I reached maturity, time ran away; when I reached old age, time flew swiftly; and very soon, as I went on my way, time disappeared."

The psalmist said: "So teach us to number our days, that we may bring wisdom into our hearts". (Psalm 90:12) And that wisdom is the Lord Jesus Christ Himself. Someone described this as follows: "Thou knowest Lord that I am growing old." And he went on to say, "The fire of my youth begins to burn without flame; somehow I tend to remember and talk about the good days that I begin to miss. I have a changeable, bossy mood, and I think that everyone must obey my orders immediately. Help me, Lord, to hide my pains and to realize my own mistakes. Make me a sweet, silent, serene person; instead of being harsh, bitter and mean. May the Lord help us to grow old with dignity! Then, in verses 9 to 11, of this 12th chapter of Ecclesiastes, we read:

"The wiser the Preacher was, the more he taught wisdom to the people. He listened, searched and composed many proverbs. The Preacher sought to find pleasant words and to write right words of truth. The words of the wise are as pricks, and the words of the teachers of the congregations, spoken by a shepherd, are as nails driven in.

In no way should we despise the wisdom of the past, nor refuse to be taught. And verse 12, says:

"Now, son, in addition to this, accept to be admonished. There is no point in writing many books; much study is fatigue for the body."

According to the writer's conclusion, education does not solve life's problems. Let us now read verse 13, in which Solomon spoke to us of the

Result of the experiment

"The end of all the speech which thou hast heard is, Fear God, and keep his commandments: for this is the whole of man."

Here the command "Fear God" stands out. This is the message of the Book of Proverbs as well as the message of this passage. In the light of the experiment conducted "under the sun", a wise attitude is to have a fear of God which means reverence, worship and obedience towards Him.

And Solomon went on to say "and keep his commandments," which implies satisfying God's conditions for salvation, at whatever age, based on faith in God. For Abel, son of Adam, it involved bringing a lamb.

For Abraham it meant believing God's promises. For the people of Israel it meant approaching God by means of a sacrifice in the tabernacle and in the temple. For us it means responding to the following invitation, "Believe in the Lord Jesus Christ, and you will be saved." (Acts 16:31)

Finally, let us read verse 14 of this last chapter 12 of Ecclesiastes.

"For God will bring every work into judgment, together with every hidden thing, whether it be good or whether it be evil."

Here it says "God will bring every work into judgment". In other words, God will judge each individual, because each one is a guilty sinner before God. Christ suffered our judgment; He died a death of judgment. Our sins are upon Christ by faith in Him, or else we will have to stand before the Great White Throne for judgment.

At the beginning of this chapter 12, we read: "Remember your Creator in the days of your youth". Why? For a very specific reason: because in the matter of salvation the chances of being saved are greater; and in the matter of service you will have something to offer to God. Statistics show that more people come to Christ when they are young. But that does not mean that older people cannot accept Christ and be saved. In our experience, we know of many, many cases of older people who begin to establish a relationship with God.

The second reason Solomon appealed especially to young men was that, in every age, they have had a lifetime of service to offer to God. In the Bible, those who offered real service, who had something to offer God, were young men. Remember Joseph, Moses, Daniel, Jeremiah, Gideon, David and Saul of Tarsus, Timothy, and so many other men and women one could name today.

There is no answer to the problems of life under the sun, Jesus Christ is the only solution. Jesus Christ is the only solution, so why not surrender to Him right now? He said in John 6:37: "If anyone comes to me, I will not cast him out. Come to Jesus Christ right now and be saved for eternity!

And so we conclude our study of this Book of Ecclesiastes. God willing in our next study, we will continue in the Old Testament and as we say goodbye today we invite you to join us in our study of the *Song of Songs*.

Conclusion

———

Solomon wrote Ecclesiastes as a warning to those who try to find joy without God. Indeed, it is impossible to live without God, for it is He who "has put eternity in their hearts" (3:11). The Solomonic pursuit of happiness through experience and philosophy leads nowhere without God. Christ did not come into the world to make human life bearable. He came to give us life "in abundance" (Jn 10:9,10). Christ remains the only shepherd, the source of all wisdom (12:11). Without Christ, therefore, any search will be vain and fruitless.

Ecclesiastes Prayer Motifs

Pray for wisdom in the search for meaning: Pray for wisdom in the search for meaning and purpose in life, inspired by the author's reflections in Ecclesiastes 1:13-14.

Confess that we depend more on God than on material achievements: Let us confess any excessive dependence on material achievements and ask God to be our true source of satisfaction, based on the warning against vanity in Ecclesiastes 2:11.

Pray for contentment in all circumstances: Pray for contentment in all circumstances, drawing on the teaching on the importance of contentment in Ecclesiastes 3:12-13.

Confess any selfish and excessive pursuit: Let us confess any selfish and excessive pursuit of pleasure and happiness and ask God to guide us toward a balanced perspective, drawing on the author's reflections in Ecclesiastes 2:1-3.

Pray for a wise approach to work and achievement: Pray for a wise approach to work and achievement, reflecting on the importance of wisdom in Ecclesiastes 2:26.

Confess any form of oppression or injustice: Let us confess any form of oppression or injustice in our lives and in the world, and ask God to enable us to work for justice, based on the reflections on oppression in Ecclesiastes 4:1.

Pray for an eternal rather than materialistic perspective: Pray for an eternal perspective rather than focusing on materialism, drawing on the teaching on the vanity of material possessions in Ecclesiastes 5:10.

Confess any unrestricted pursuit of pleasure: Let us confess any unrestricted pursuit of pleasure and ask God to guide us toward a balanced life, drawing inspiration from the reflections on pleasure in Ecclesiastes 7:2-4.

Ask for discernment in human relationships: Pray for discernment in our human relationships, drawing on the reflections on relationships in Ecclesiastes 4:9-12.

Give thanks for God's grace in the midst of vanity: Let us give thanks for God's grace in the midst of the vanity and uncertainty of life, inspired by the author's conclusion in Ecclesiastes 12:13-14.

Don't miss out!

Visit the website below and you can sign up to receive emails whenever Bible Sermons publishes a new book. There's no charge and no obligation.

https://books2read.com/r/B-A-MZBS-KTOLF

Connecting independent readers to independent writers.

Did you love *Bible Class for Adults and Youth: Beginner's Guide: Ecclesiastes*? Then you should read *Bible Class for Youth and Adults: Beginner's Guide: The Pentateuch*[1] by Bible Sermons!

Bible study series chapter by chapter, ideal for young people and adults.

In general terms, it can be stated that the Pentateuch begins with the creation of the universe and concludes with the death of Moses. Through these books, the history of Israel, the people chosen by God according to various religious doctrines, is narrated.

The Pentateuch is considered essential to understand the Bible as a whole. According to believers, it contains divine revelation to the chosen people and reflections on God's purpose for humanity.

---

1. https://books2read.com/u/3GJXka

2. https://books2read.com/u/3GJXka

Historically, the Pentateuch is significant because it recounts the history of humanity, even though it focuses on God's chosen people. It is important to remember that the biblical texts possess a breadth and depth that allow their teachings to apply to our lives, regardless of time and place; *they are stories that transcend time and space barriers, with great teachings and applications for life.*

Also by Bible Sermons

A Collection of Biblical Sermons
The Power of Great Gospel Words
The Power of Prayer: Men Ought Always to Pray
The Power of the Single Life in Christ
Analyzing The Power of a Life in Christ

Bible Characters Collection
Analyzing Biblical Scenes: 62 Inspiring Christian Teachings from the Old Testament

BIBLE CLASS FROM SCRATCH
Bible Class for Youth and Adults: Beginner's Guide: Genesis
Bible Class for Youth and Adults: Beginner's Guide: Exodus
Bible Class for Youth and Adults: Beginner's Guide: Leviticus
Bible Class for Youth and Adults: Beginner's Guide: Numbers
Bible Class for Youth and Adults: Beginner's Guide: Deuteronomy
Bible Class for Adults and Youth: Beginner's Guide: Joshua
Bible Class for Adults and Youth: Beginner's Guide: Judges
Bible Class for Adults and Youth: Beginner's Guide: Ruth
Bible Class for Adults and Youth: Beginner's Guide: 1 Samuel

Notes in the New Testament

Overflying The Bible

Chronological Prophecy: Things That Will Happen on Earth
Bible Study: Genesis 1. Creation in Six Days

PROPHETIC PROFILE

Prophetic Profile: The Last Week, The Great Tribulation

STUDY FROM SCRATCH

Bible Class for Youth and Adults: Beginner's Guide: The Pentateuch

Teaching in the Bible class

Sunday School Lessons: 182 Bible Stories
Bible Class for Beginners: 50 Beautiful Lessons
Lessons for Sunday School: 62 Biblical Characters
How to Teach in Sunday School: A Guide for Bible Class Teachers

Teaching in the Bible Classroom

Studying Teaching in the Bible Classroom: A Teacher's Guide

The Education of Labor in the Bible

Analyzing the Education of Labor in Genesis: The Purpose of Life on Earth
Analyzing the Teaching of Labor in Exodus: From Slavery to Liberation
Analyzing the Labor Education in Leviticus: The Spirit of the Law at Work

Analyzing Labor Education in John's Gospel
Analyzing Labor Education in the Acts of the Apostles
Analyzing Labor Education in the Epistle to the Romans
Analyzing Labor Education in the Epistle to the Corinthians
Analyzing Labor Education in the Epistles of Galatians, Ephesians and Philippians
Analyzing Labor Education in the Epistles to Colossians, Philemon and Thessalonians
Analyzing Labor Education in the Pastoral Letters: Timothy and Titus
Analyzing Labor Education in the General Letters and the Apocalypse
Analyzing Labor Education in the Four Gospels and the Acts
Analyzing Labor Education in the Epistles of the Apostle Paul
Analyzing Labor Education in the New Testament of the Bible
Analyzing Labor Education in Pentateuch
Analyzing Labor Education in the Historical Books: Applying the Bible to Practical Labor
Analyzing Labor Education in the Pentateuch and Books Historical
God's Guide for Work: Discovering God's Will for a Particular Job
Analyzing Labor Education in Poetic Books
Analyzing Labor Education in the Prophetic Books of the Bible
Analyzing Labor Education in the 12 Prophets of the Bible
Analyzing Labor Education in the Old Testament

Standalone
Analyzing Notes in the 4 Gospels: Commentary Biblical
Analyzing What is to Come: God's Prophecies
The Prophetic Book Abdias: The Destruction of Edom
Bible Class for Youth and Adults: Beginner's Guide: I Don't Let Myself be Weetened

About the Author

This bible study series is perfect for Christians of any level, from children to youth to adults. It provides an engaging and interactive way to learn the Bible, with activities and discussion topics that will help deepen your understanding of scripture and strengthen your faith. Whether you're a beginner or an experienced Christian, this series will help you grow in your knowledge of the Bible and strengthen your relationship with God. Led by brothers with exemplary testimonies and extensive knowledge of scripture, who congregate in the name of the Lord Jesus Christ throughout the world.